GARDEN LIBRARY
PLANTING FIELDS ARBORETUM

Sunset

BEST KIDS™ GARDEN BOOK

By the Sunset Editors

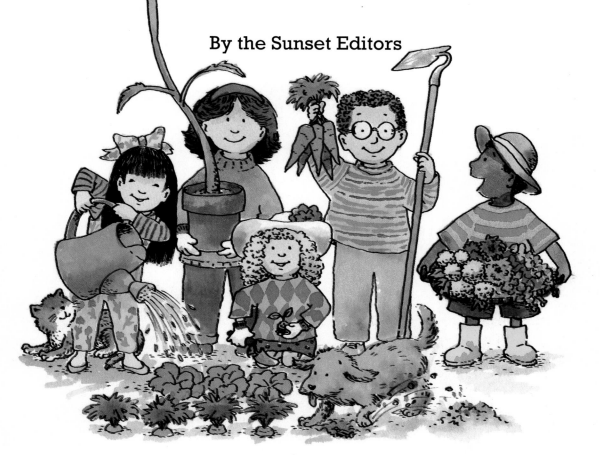

Sunset Publishing Corporation ■ Menlo Park, California

Book Editor
Phyllis Elving

Research & Text
Lance Walheim
Patricia Parrott West
Sally Wittman

Coordinating Editor
Suzanne Normand Eyre

Art Direction
Susan Bryant

Illustration
Sandra Forrest
Best Kids art

Viki Marugg
Botanical art

Design
Katherine Tillotson

Photography
Scott Atkinson: 7, 9, 10, 15, 18, 21, 24, 25, 26, 29, 31, 33, 37, 39, 45, 49, 51, 52, 53, 54, 55, 60, 63, 64, 71, 75, 80, 85, 91, 93.
Saxon Holt: 89 top. **Stephen Marley:** 82 bottom right, 92. **Ells Marugg:** 87 top, 88 bottom, 89 bottom, 90 bottom. **Jack McDowell:** 76 top. **Norman A. Plate:** 82 bottom left, 83, 88 top. **Michael Thompson:** 87 bottom. **Darrow M. Watt:** 58, 70, 73 bottom, 74, 76 bottom, 90 top. **Nik Zurek:** 72.

Photo Styling
JoAnn Masaoka Van Atta: 7, 10, 15, 18, 21, 24, 25, 26, 29, 31, 33, 37, 39, 45, 49, 51, 52, 54, 55, 60, 64, 85, 91.

Join the Best Kids in the Garden

Grab a shovel, grab a trowel—it's time to get growing! Planning and planting your own garden is one of the most rewarding things you can do. Plant it in the ground, or plant it in pots or even a jar. Grow food to eat, flowers to look at, or plants that are just fun to touch.

We've included step-by-step instructions for getting your garden ready, planting it, and taking care of your plants. Follow these guides to good gardening, and you'll be a best kid gardener in no time! To get you started, we suggest lots of plants that are especially fun to grow, and we tell you what to do to grow them.

You'll find lots of special projects to add to the fun of gardening. You can try drying flowers and making pictures with them, or growing a little garden from kitchen leftovers. You can make a rain gauge, raise worms, carve a potato printing stamp, and even grow a green-bean tent!

Many people helped to make this book. We would especially like to thank Cynthia Overbeck Bix for researching and writing many of the special features. Our thanks, too, to Nathan Armstrong, Jessica Baukol, Nathan Kramer, and Jessica Reichert for giving us the kids' point of view. And finally, we are grateful to the Grand Lake Ace Garden Center in Oakland for the use of props for photographs.

Editor, Sunset Books: Elizabeth L. Hogan

First printing September 1992

Copyright © 1992, Sunset Publishing Corporation, Menlo Park, CA 94025. First edition. World rights reserved. No part of this publication may be reproduced by any mechanical, photographic, or electronic process, or in the form of a phonographic recording, nor may it be stored in a retrieval system, transmitted, or otherwise copied for public or private use without prior written permission from the publisher. Library of Congress Catalog Card Number: 92-81024. ISBN 0-376-03076-3. Lithographed in the United States.

CONTENTS

Special Features

DIGGING IN

Did you ever want to be a magician? A garden is full of magic. Tiny seeds buried in the soil turn into plants pushing their way up toward the sunlight. First you see them just barely peeking through the soil, and then suddenly they are getting bigger every day! You can be a garden magician and make it all happen—just become a gardener!

As a gardener you will discover many things. The first time you eat a homegrown tomato you'll be amazed at how much better it tastes than store-bought tomatoes. A fresh ear of corn picked right off the stalk tastes so good that it will make you feel like singing!

Discover how much fun it is to carve a jack o' lantern from a pumpkin that you have grown yourself. Or grow some giant sunflowers and find out how it feels to have the tallest flowers in the neighborhood. In fact, you can grow zillions of flowers! Plant a row of sweet peas—they're pretty, and they smell good, too. You'll be able to give bouquets to all your neighbors.

You can even start a little garden from kitchen scraps without spending a penny. That's right! You can grow a plant from an avocado seed or the top of a carrot—read how to do it on pages 64 and 65.

You can garden anywhere!

You don't need to live in the country or have a big yard to be a gardener. You can have a garden just about anywhere, any time, even if you live in an apartment in the city and are snowed in! If you don't have anyplace to plant a garden in the ground, a container on a porch or a deck will work fine. Or you can have a row of pots indoors on a windowsill. You can even make a garden in a jar. There's almost always *some* way to have some kind of garden.

You might want to plan a garden with other members of your family, or with some friends or neighbors or your class at school. Or it might be a project you want to do by yourself. You may need help from grown-ups for some things, but you can do most of the jobs yourself.

BE A SAFE GARDENER!
To have a good time gardening, you need to stay safe. Here are some important safety rules.

Plant safety. Never eat the leaves, fruit, seeds, or other parts of any plant if you don't know for sure it is safe. Many ordinary plants have some poisonous parts. Even if it's okay to eat one part of a plant, another part might make you sick.

Chemical safety. When any gardening chemical is being used, adults should supervise. Children should *not* use poisonous chemicals. Organic methods are safest for kids—and kindest to the environment. Ask an adult to help you use them.

*A pig pot makes
a friendly home for
a mint plant.*

Plants give us fresh air & food

Gardening isn't just fun—it's also good for the earth
when you help plants grow. Plants send oxygen into
the air as they grow, and that's good for all of us. We
all need oxygen to breathe. When we plant a tree we
are planting a giant air freshener!

It might surprise you to know how many ways
plants help us. You know about the vegetables and
fruits we get from plants and the wood we get from
trees. But did you know that bread, noodles, rice, sugar,
cooking oil, chewing gum, and chocolate are all made
from parts of plants? Clothing, rope, fertilizers, and
dyes may come from plants, too. And lots of lotions,
shampoos, and medicines are made from plants.

What do plants need to grow?

Plants need food, water, air, and sunlight in order to grow. It's your job as a gardener to make sure your plants get the things they need.

Plants get most of their food from the soil, which contains minerals such as nitrogen and phosphorus that they need. These nutrients are in the water that plants suck up from the soil.

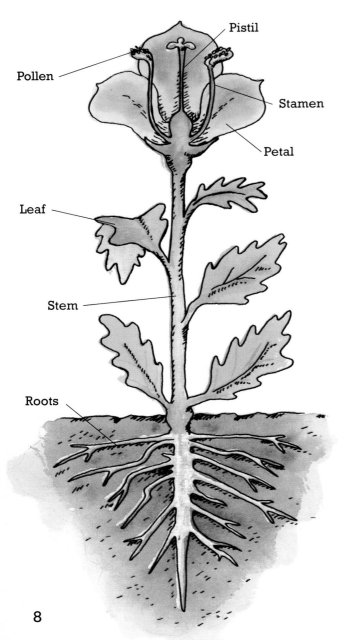

This is how plants get food for themselves and at the same time help make the air good for us to breathe:

■ The roots take in nutrients (food) by drinking water from the soil.

■ The stem carries the water to the leaves.

■ The leaves make plant food by mixing nutrients in the water with carbon dioxide from the air. This process is called "photosynthesis." It takes chlorophyll and sunlight to make photosynthesis work. (Chlorophyll is what makes leaves green.)

■ As the plant makes food, it gives off oxygen, which all other living things need in order to breathe. And then people and animals breathe out carbon dioxide, which the plants need.

But how do plants make more plants? Inside the flower part of each plant, something called pollen is produced—the powdery yellow stuff you see inside the blossom. Pollen from one plant is carried to another plant by insects and birds, and by the wind. When flowers are "pollinated" this way, seeds can grow inside them. These seeds are scattered by the wind and by birds and other animals—and by people. When the seeds find a resting place in the soil, they grow into new plants.

Seeds behind Glass

We don't usually get to see a plant sprouting from a seed—it happens underground. But here is a way you can watch this amazing process.

1 Fit a folded paper towel or a piece of blotter paper into a jar so that it reaches all the way around. You can stuff paper towels into the middle to hold the folded towel or blotter paper in place against the side of the jar, if you need to.

2 Push the seeds down between the glass and the paper. (If you need to, use a spoon handle to press the paper away from the glass just enough to let you slip in the seeds.) Space the seeds evenly around the jar, halfway between top and bottom.

3 Pour a little water into the jar. After the paper has soaked up enough water to make it damp, pour out any extra water.

4 Now put the jar in a sunny window. Check it every day, and add a little water if the paper starts to dry out. The seeds will begin to swell as they soak up water, and in a few days to a week or so you'll see them split and send out little roots.

Soon stems will start to grow upward from each seed, and little seed leaves called "cotyledons" will appear. Finally a pair of true leaves will grow. When a seedling has two pairs of true leaves, you can try planting it in a pot of soil, if you want to.

WHAT YOU NEED

Clean glass jar

Paper towels or desk blotter paper (sold at stationery stores)

4 or 5 large seeds (beans, peas, or other kinds)

Spoon

Pea seeds

9

Spading fork

Shovel

Kid-size shovel

Kid-size rake

Spade

Hand cultivator

Kid-size hoe

Trowel

Weeder

Pruning shears

Tools & Equipment for Gardeners

What gardening tools do you need? It depends on the kind of garden you have. Do you have a big garden that will need a lot of digging, or a tiny patch of soil? Or do you have a pot garden? A spade or shovel, a rake, a hoe, and maybe a spading fork are the most important big tools for a garden in the ground. For pots, all you need is a trowel or other digging tool—even an old spoon.

It's a lot easier to work with tools if they are the right size for you. That may mean kid-size tools. You can buy sturdy kid-size tools from some hardware stores, garden stores, and mail-order catalogs. Check around—there is quite a range of prices.

To get a good "fit," try handling both kid-size tools and adult tools at the store. What feels comfortable? Adult-size hand tools, such as trowels, are usually fine for kids. Just be sure the handles feel okay.

Here are some kinds of garden tools and what each one is used for.

Rake. Some rakes are used to break up lumps in the soil and make the soil smooth. Others are used to gather up leaves and clippings.

Hoe. Used to break up soil, chop weeds, and make planting furrows.

Shovel. Used to dig and move soil.

Spade. A shovel with a square end, used to dig soil to an even depth and to move soil.

Spading fork. Used to dig and break up lumps in soil.

Hand cultivator. Used to dig out weeds and break up soil in a small area.

Trowel. Used to dig small planting holes, to dig out weeds, and to scoop up soil.

Pruning shears. Used to trim off leaves, branches, and fruit.

Weeder. Used to dig up weeds.

What else will you need?

Every gardener needs something to water plants with—a hose with a spray nozzle, or a watering can with a sprinkler attachment (called a "rose"). A plant mister or spray bottle is helpful for gently watering seeds in trays or pots.

For big outdoor gardens, it's nice to have a wheelbarrow or a wagon for hauling soil, compost, and clippings.

For yourself, be sure you have old clothes and shoes (or rubber boots) that can get dirty. Sunscreen and a hat will keep you from getting sunburned. Gardening gloves will protect your hands from prickly plants.

Safety with tools

Talk over with your parents or adult helper which tools you're allowed to use by yourself. Always follow these safety rules when you handle tools:

■ Carry hand tools with sharp edges pointing down. (Don't run with a tool!) When you aren't using them, shove them into the dirt, handle up. Put them away when you've finished for the day.

■ Shove long-handled tools into the soil, handles up, when you're not using them. Put them away when you've finished for the day. Don't lean tools against glass, and don't lay them down on the ground with sharp edges pointing up.

Taking care of your tools

Store your tools in a safe, dry place. To keep metal tools from getting rusty, scrape off the dirt and every so often rub the metal part with a little oil. (You can use any lubricating oil, even motor oil—but not cooking oil.)

A Short Dictionary of Gardening Words

When you read gardening catalogs, garden books, seed packets, or signs at nurseries or garden centers, you may come across some words you don't know. Here are some of the special words that gardeners often use.

Annual. A plant that completes its whole growth cycle in one year or less—sprouting, growing, blooming, making seeds, and dying. Its roots do not live to make a new plant the following year. A marigold is an annual.

Bud. A part of a plant that will grow to be a blossom or new leaves.

Bulb. A thickened underground plant stem that stores food during its dormant season and then makes a new plant during the growing season. Plants that grow from bulbs, such as daffodils, are also called bulbs.

Some plants that aren't really bulbs grow just the same way, from other kinds of underground stems—like crocus (which grow from "corms") and some kinds of iris (which grow from "rhizomes").

Cell-pack. A shallow planting container that is divided into small compartments to hold seedlings.

Compost. Kitchen and garden scraps that are allowed to decay to make a material rich in nutrients for plants.

Cultivate. To dig the soil around plants to let air in and to remove weeds.

Cutting. A piece of a plant that is cut off and used to grow a new plant. Sometimes cuttings are called "slips."

Dormant. Resting, not active. A plant that is dormant is resting between growing seasons.

Drainage. A way for water to move through the soil. If water can't drain away from a plant's roots, the plant will drown.

Fertilizer. Nutrients added to the soil to make plants grow better. Another name for fertilizer is "plant food." Some fertilizers are organic, and some are man-made chemicals.

Flat. A shallow tray in which plants are grown from seeds.

Forcing. Making plants blossom or grow sooner than normal. Sometimes bulbs are forced by growing them indoors.

Furrow. A narrow ditch for planting or watering.

Germinate. To sprout, or begin to grow. When a seed germinates, it sends up its first green shoot.

Hybrid. A new plant created by crossing two different plants together.

Insecticide (pesticide). A substance used to kill insects. Many insecticides are poisonous chemicals.

Mature. Completely grown or fully developed. A mature plant is a grown-up plant.

Mulch. A covering for the soil to keep it from drying out, to keep weeds from growing, and sometimes to keep fruit or vegetables from rotting when they touch the ground.

Straw mulch

Nursery. A place where plants are grown and sold. A garden store.

Organic. Made from things that have been alive or that come from a living thing, either plant or animal. "Organic gardening" means gardening without man-made chemicals.

Peat. A spongy material made from decayed moss dug from the earth, sometimes added to garden soil.

Perennial. A plant that grows back year after year from the same roots. A carnation is a perennial.

pH. A measurement to tell how "acid" or "alkaline" soil is. (See page 20.) Gardeners use this information to tell them if they need to add things to their soil.

Photosynthesis. The process by which green plants use sunlight to make food for themselves and to give off oxygen.

Pollinate. To move pollen from flower stamens to flower pistils so that seeds can begin growing. ("Stamens" and "pistils" are parts inside the blossom—see the picture on page 8.) Usually plants are pollinated by wind or by insects.

Propagate. To make more plants, for instance by growing them from seeds or cuttings.

Prune. To cut off branches or leaves—a plant "haircut." Plants are pruned to make room for new growth, to get rid of unhealthy parts, or to give them a certain shape.

Seedling. A young plant from a recently germinated seed.

Shoot. New growth that comes from a seed or a main stem of a plant.

Soil. Dirt—the part of the earth's surface in which plants grow. "Potting soil" is a special mixture of materials for planting in containers.

Sow. To scatter or plant seeds.

Sprout. To begin to grow—to send up a shoot. Another word for sprout is "germinate."

Till. To dig or plow soil for planting, smoothing out lumps and letting air in.

Transplant. To plant again in a different place or container. A plant that is replanted this way is also called a transplant.

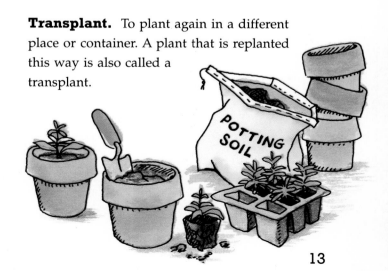

Creating Your Own Garden Journal

WHAT YOU NEED

3-ring notebook with plastic cover

Decorations for the cover

Clear plastic adhesive shelf paper

Notebook paper

Optional extras: zippered 3-hole plastic pencil pouch, plastic index tabs, wall calendar, 3-hole pocket pages

A lot happens in a garden. You think and plan, dig and plant. You watch things grow. Sometimes you just sit and daydream. One way to remember all these things is to write them down in a journal. You can use any notebook as a journal, or you can decorate a special one yourself.

One way to decorate the front of your journal is to glue on pictures of flowers, fruits, and vegetables that you cut out of magazines, seed catalogs, or old greeting cards. Or you could draw your own pictures, or use stickers of flowers, birds, and butterflies. Keep your decorations from getting wet or dirty by covering them with a piece of clear plastic adhesive shelf paper. (You can buy this in rolls or by the yard at a hardware store or variety store.) The directions are printed on the back of the paper, but you may want some adult help—it's a little tricky to handle the sticky paper.

What goes inside

Your notebook can begin with a map of your garden, showing where you planted everything. It doesn't have to be fancy—just draw the shapes of the planting areas as if you were looking down from above. Next year, you'll be able to look at your map to remember what you planted in your garden this year. If you want to, you can add some photos or drawings of your garden.

The rest of your journal can be divided by months. You could use plastic index tabs to label the months, or pages from a calendar. Here are some things you could write down for each month:

- What seeds did you plant? (When?)

- What else did you plant in the garden? (When? Where?)

- What seeds sprouted? (When?)

- What plants bloomed? (When? What color were they?)

- Did you pick any vegetables and fruits? (When? How many?)

- How tall were your full-grown plants? (Did they have enough room?)

- What days did you water?

- Did you fertilize any plants? (What kind of fertilizer did you use?)

- Did you prune any plants?

- What garden visitors did you see? (Birds, bees, butterflies, others?)

- Did you have problems with garden pests? (What did you do?)

- What was the weather like? (When did it rain? Was there frost? What were the highest and lowest temperatures?)

Leave an extra page or two for each month to write down thoughts and ideas or to draw pictures of your garden. You could keep pencils and markers in a zippered pencil pouch right in your notebook. If you want to, add some pocket pages for things like seed packets and magazine clippings.

PLANTING TIME

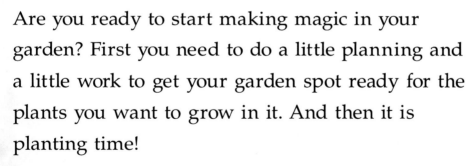

Are you ready to start making magic in your garden? First you need to do a little planning and a little work to get your garden spot ready for the plants you want to grow in it. And then it is planting time!

Do you know where your garden is going to be? Will it be in the ground or in pots? The perfect place for a garden in the ground would get sun most of the day and have good soil without rocks and weeds. It would be on level ground, and there would be a faucet nearby. Of course, we don't all have the perfect place. But don't worry—there are lots of things you can do to make a garden spot better.

With a container garden, it's even easier. Bad soil can't stop you—you can buy potting soil. And you can set your pots where they get the best sun.

You don't need a lot of space. Maybe you could use a corner of a grown-up's garden, or maybe you can find some room in your yard that you can turn into your own garden. Even a space 3 or 4 feet long on each side will let you grow several kinds of plants.

Looking for clues

Before you plant anything, you need to find out some things about your garden spot. That's part of being a good gardener!

Sun. How much sunlight will your garden get each day? Most vegetables like to be in the sun at least 6 hours a day, but there are shade-loving plants, too.

Shade. Are there fences, buildings, or trees that make shade in your garden? You don't want to plant sun-loving plants where it's shady most of the time.

Which way is north? If you plant tall plants such as corn on the north side of your garden, they won't shade the short plants. Ask a grown-up helper which way is north, or use a compass to figure it out.

Frost. When is the last spring frost where you live? When is the first frost of the fall or winter? The time between these two dates is the growing season for your area.

Many kinds of plants will freeze to death in a frost, so it's important to know your average last spring frost date. That means that where you live it usually isn't freezing cold after that date. If your adult garden helpers don't know, you can ask at a nursery or call your county Cooperative Extension Service or Farm Adviser. Look in the phone book under county government listings.

When you know your spring frost date, you can figure out when to start planting things. If you live where winters are mild, you might not have to worry about frost at all.

Marigolds and sweet alyssum in a barrel garden

Start a Worm Box

Have a little respect for the lowly earthworm. It helps your garden grow! Worms nibble away at dead leaves and other garden "leftovers," and these add nutrients to your garden soil when they are digested. And worms wiggle through the soil, making space for air to get in. That's good for plants, too. Why not start a worm box to add more worms to your garden?

1 Line your box with the black garbage bag. Let the extra hang over the edges.

2 Scoop in soil to a couple of inches from the top of the box.

3 Add several handfuls of garden and kitchen scraps and mix everything together with your trowel.

4 Moisten the soil with your spray bottle. Then set the box in a cool, dry spot out of the sun for a few days. (Put the lid or screening on to keep animals out. You can use rocks to hold down the screening.)

5 Carefully dig up 6 or 8 big worms. It's easiest to find them in damp soil.

6 Stir the soil in the box and moisten it if it has dried out. Then put the worms on top and cover the box again. (If you're using a lid, poke air holes in it.)

Keep the soil in the box moist but not soaked, and add more cut-up garden and kitchen scraps every week or two. After a few weeks, carefully stir the soil. Have you grown more worms? If so, you can put a couple in your garden. You can also add a few scoops of the worm box soil to your garden. Do this every month or so—just be sure to add some new soil to the box.

WHAT YOU NEED

Large, sturdy cardboard box

Lid or wire screening to cover the box

Black plastic garbage bag

Garden soil or potting soil

Garden and kitchen leftovers, cut into little pieces (weeds, dead leaves, vegetable and fruit peelings)

Trowel

Spray bottle of water

Earthworms from your garden (or from a fishing bait store)

The Real "Dirt" on Soil

Soil provides food for your plants. If it isn't just right, you can usually fix it. But first you have to know what's wrong with it.

Some soil is kind of heavy and sticky, like clay. Some soil is more like sand. The very best soil is in between—it feels crumbly but it doesn't just fall apart when you squeeze it into a ball.

Water doesn't drain through clay soil very well, so plant roots can end up sitting in water. They don't like that! But water might drain through sandy soil *too* fast, so plants could dry out. The surprising thing is that you can usually fix clay soil and sandy soil the same way—by adding organic material.

Organic material is something that used to be alive (like peat moss or wood chips) or that came from something alive (like cow manure). One of the best kinds of organic material is compost, and you can make that yourself by recycling scraps from your garden and kitchen! (See how on page 22.)

You can get different kinds of organic material at the nursery, too. Even good soil gets better when you add some organic material to it.

How does your soil rate?

Another fact that is helpful to know is your soil's pH—its acid rating. Most plants like soil that's not too "acid" and not too "alkaline." If you live in a very rainy place, your soil might be acid. If you live where there's not much rain at all, your soil might be alkaline.

You can ask at a nursery or call your county's Cooperative Extension Service to find out if soil in your

Testing soil for pH

area has pH problems. If it does, you can do an easy experiment to see whether you need to fix your soil's pH. Nurseries sell pH test kits. Just follow the directions to collect a little soil in a tube and add a chemical to it. Then compare the color in the tube with the chart in the kit, and you'll be able to see what your soil's pH is.

If your soil turns out to be very acid, you can put lime into it to make it less acid. If it is too alkaline, you can put in some sulfur. These things are sold at nurseries. (See step 3 on page 23.)

Look out for lead

There's another kind of soil test that's a good idea to do where kids are going to garden, and that's a lead test. Lead is a mineral that is toxic—poisonous. It's especially dangerous for children. Paint and gasoline used to contain lead, so if you live near old buildings or where there's a lot of traffic, your soil could have lead in it.

A soil-testing laboratory can test for lead if you send in a little sample of soil. If the test shows that your soil has too much lead, you shouldn't garden in it, or even play in it. But you can still grow plants in containers. Just buy potting soil.

To find a lab, you can look in the Yellow Pages of the phone book under "Soil testing" or call your county Cooperative Extension Service, which is listed in the phone book under county government offices. The lab report will tell you how much lead is in your soil, but it may not explain whether that amount is dangerous. Call your Cooperative Extension Service or the lab for help in understanding the report.

Lab tests can be expensive. If you can't find anyplace that will do a low-cost test for lead, you can try one of the labs listed on page 95.

The Magic Compost Pile

Making compost is almost like doing a magic trick. You turn a pile of scraps into food for your plants!

Making compost takes some time, because you have to let the scraps decay until you can't tell what they are any-more. It takes at least a month, so start early. You can buy a little to use until yours is ready. Compost can be mixed in with soil to make plants grow better, or it can be spread on top of the soil around your plants.

What can you throw onto your compost pile? Just think of your plants as glorious garbage eaters that like these things:

■ Garden scraps, such as dried or fresh grass clippings, leaves and small stems, and young weeds that haven't gone to seed (but no bermuda grass—it will sprout up everywhere).

■ Organic kitchen scraps (vegetable and fruit scraps cut into small pieces, coffee grounds, used teabags, eggshells—but no meat, bones, or anything oily).

Don't use branches, corncobs, or other hard things unless you have a compost shredder to chop them up into little pieces. They take too long to decay.

Start your compost pile where it won't get in anyone's way. Throw kitchen and garden leftovers into a pile 3 or 4 feet wide. When the pile is 3 or 4 feet tall, either cover it with a thin layer of manure (from cows or other farm animals) or sprinkle on 2 handfuls of nitrogen fertilizer from the nursery.

Water the pile and cover it with a piece of black plastic held down with some stones. Now you let it "cook." It actually will get hot inside! Once a week, take off the cover and mix up the heap really well with a spading fork. (This takes some muscle—you may want help.) If your compost seems to be "working"—if it's nice and warm—you can just water it again so it is as damp as a squeezed-out sponge. If it doesn't seem warm, add more manure or nitrogen fertilizer. Then put the cover back on.

If your compost smells bad, you've probably watered it too much. When your heap is dark and crumbly and you can't recognize the different things you put in, it's ready to use.

Get Ready, Get Set, Dig!

Getting your soil prepared is the most important thing you do to get your garden off to a good start. It is hard work, but you don't have to do it all in one day.

Start when the ground is warm enough in the spring to be dug easily. The soil should be crumbly—not dry and hard, but not too wet.

1 Dig or pull out all the grass and weeds. Be sure to get the roots, or they'll grow back in a jiffy.

2 Use a spade, spading fork, or shovel to chop up the lumps in your soil and let air in. Dig down about 1 foot, or at least as deep as your tool goes. Turn the soil over as you dig, and take out any rocks you find.

3 Is your soil's pH too high or too low? (Read about pH on pages 20 and 21.) Sprinkle on lime (ground limestone) if your soil is too acid or sulfur if it is too alkaline. (Ask at the nursery how much you need.)

4 Spread on some organic matter to put more nutrients in the soil and make it loose and fluffy. If you've made compost, spread it 2 or 3 inches deep over your soil. Otherwise, you can get compost or another organic material, such as leaf mold or shredded bark, at the nursery.

5 Add some organic fertilizer (such as aged manure) or a complete chemical fertilizer. "Complete" means it contains the three most important plant nutrients: nitrogen, phosphorus, and potassium. Follow the directions on the package or ask someone at the nursery how much to use.

6 Use a shovel or spading fork to mix everything together—your soil and anything you've added.

7 Rake the soil smooth.

Pick Your Plants

Have you decided what to plant in your garden? The chapter "Fun Plants to Grow" starting on page 67 can help you choose plants that are especially good for kids to grow. If you aren't sure what will grow best where you live, the people who work at nurseries can help you.

Once you have decided what you want to grow, you can make a garden plan. Draw a map of your garden showing what you will plant in each part of it. Seed packets or gardening books will tell you how much space you need for each kind of plant.

Shopping for plants

At the nursery, you can buy packets of seeds, or you can buy seedlings—baby plants. Look in the "Fun Plants to Grow" chapter to find out whether a certain plant is best to start from seeds or seedlings, or ask someone at the garden store.

Seedlings are often sold in something called a "cell-pack" or "six-pack," which is a little tray divided into compartments. Look for sturdy-looking seedlings with a nice green color and at least four leaves. Don't buy seedlings if their roots are crowding out of the container, or if they look tall and spindly and lean to one side.

You can also buy bigger plants. (These cost more.) And some plants grow from bulbs instead of seeds or seedlings. Bulbs are fat underground stems that are often shaped like onions. Onions are bulbs, too!

Seedling

Seeds

Plant in 4-inch pot

Bulbs

Seedlings from Scratch

Growing your own seedlings indoors from seeds is more than just fun—it's smart! Seeds are cheaper to buy than nursery seedlings, and they come in more varieties.

Look for containers at the nursery or around your own house. Some ideas are plastic or peat cell-packs (six-packs), planting trays ("flats"), small clay pots, egg cartons, milk cartons cut in half lengthwise, and yogurt or cottage cheese containers. Punch drainage holes in the bottoms of homemade containers.

Start your seeds 6 to 8 weeks before the plants should go into your outdoor garden. Here's what you do:

1 Fill the containers with potting soil, leaving enough room for watering.

2 Read your seed package. How deep should you plant your seeds? Poke holes that deep with a pencil or your finger.

3 Drop seeds into the holes.

4 Pat the soil gently but firmly over the seeds.

5 Gently water the containers. A spray bottle works well.

Now place your containers in a warm, bright spot while you wait for the seeds to sprout. Water them whenever the soil starts to get dry—seeds won't grow if they dry out. But soil that is soaking wet can kill seedlings, too. *Moist* soil is ideal.

When your seedlings have two pairs of leaves, pull out any that are closer than the seed packet says they should be. You can also start getting them used to outdoor conditions. Take them outside for just a few hours the first day, then bring them back inside. Each day leave them out a little longer. In about a week they will be ready to plant in the ground or in bigger containers outdoors.

Planting Your Garden in the Ground

Once your soil is prepared, you are ready to start planting. You can plant in rows, which makes it easy to weed and take care of your plants. Or you can push soil up into planting mounds. (Don't make your mounds wider than about 3 feet, or you won't be able to reach the middle.) For that matter, you can arrange your plants in your garden any way you want to! Some kinds of seeds can just be scattered and then covered with a little soil. This is called "broadcasting" seed.

Decide how you are going to water your garden. If you are going to make watering furrows, dig them before you plant your seeds or seedlings in rows between them. (See page 36.)

To make a planting row. Poke a garden stake or a stick into the ground at each end of where you want the row to be. Then use your finger, a stick, or a hoe to draw a planting line—a furrow—between the two stakes. If you want your rows to be exactly straight, you can tie a string between the stakes and draw your line right under the string. But you don't have to.

Your seed packets will tell you how far apart to make your rows. If you want to be able to walk between rows, add at least 12 extra inches for a path.

Planting your seeds

If you are starting with seeds, here's what to do.

1 Read the seed package. How deep should you plant your seeds? Make your planting furrow that deep, or poke holes that deep in your mounds.

2 Drop seeds along the furrow or in your planting holes a couple of inches apart, or twice as close as the seed packet says they should be. (They will have to be thinned out later, but this way it won't matter if some

Lima bean

Pumpkin

Corn

Watermelon

Pea

Cosmos

Radish

Poppy

Some seeds are big, others tiny.

of them don't grow.) If your seeds are too tiny to plant one by one, sprinkle them all along the row, or sprinkle several into each hole.

3 Pat the soil gently but firmly over the seeds.

4 Water your seeds with a fine spray. Don't flood them—you could wash them away! Wait awhile and water them again.

While you're waiting for your seeds to sprout, keep the soil moist but not soaked. When your seedlings have two pairs of leaves, you need to thin them. Thinning means pulling out any that are growing too close. Otherwise their roots won't have enough room. Your seed package will tell you how much space should be between them.

Planting seedlings

Here's how to get seedlings into the ground safely.

1 Dig holes as deep as the root ball (the part of the seedling that is in soil)

and twice as wide. (See the drawing below.) Space them the right distance apart. Check a seed packet or a garden book to see how far apart they should be, or ask at a nursery.

2 Water the holes gently.

3 Take seedlings out of cell-packs by pushing on the bottom. For seedlings in flats, slice straight down through the soil with an old table knife or spatula to separate seedlings, then lift them out. If you are using peat cell-packs, just pull the sections apart—you plant the pot along with the seedling.

4 Stretch out the roots a little bit, or soak peat pots in a pan of water.

5 Set each seedling in its planting hole and fill the hole with soil.

6 Press down gently on the soil around the seedling to make a shallow watering basin—a little moat to catch water so it will sink down to the roots.

7 Water your seedlings gently and then water again an hour later.

If you plant bulbs carefully, many kinds will bloom year after year! Just make sure you plant each bulb at the right depth in the soil, and make sure you plant it right side up.

Nurseries and gardening books have information about how deep each kind of bulb should be planted. Here are some general rules to help you:

■ Big bulbs should be planted deeper than small ones. You usually can't go wrong if you plant a bulb in a hole that is 2 to 3 times deeper than the length of the bulb from top to bottom. So a bulb that is 2 inches long should be planted in a hole 4 to 6 inches deep.

■ If you don't know which end of a bulb is which, look for dried-up roots on one end—that's the bottom. The top is usually pointed.

Make a planting hole 2 to 3 times deeper than the bulb

Read more about bulbs on pages 82 and 83. To plant yours, follow these steps:

1 Dig a hole as deep as you need for the kind of bulb you are planting.

2 Sprinkle 1 teaspoon of bulb food (or as much as the directions say) into the hole and mix it into the soil. (You can buy a bag of bulb food at the nursery.)

3 Set the bulb in the hole, right side up, and fill up the hole with soil.

4 Water the soil.

NAMETAGS FOR PLANTS

Plant labels will help you remember what you've planted where. You can buy plant markers at the nursery, use wooden sticks from ice cream bars, or cover seed packets with clear packaging tape and fasten them to sticks or garden stakes. Use permanent marking pens so that the writing won't disappear when the labels get wet!

HELLO! MY NAME IS DAFFODIL

HELLO! MY NAME IS

*Succulent plants
growing in
a seashell*

Planting a Container Garden

You can grow all sorts of plants in containers, indoors or out. To get some ideas, turn to the "Fun Plants to Grow" chapter beginning on page 67.

Your containers might be big or little. Half-barrels sold at garden stores make nice big containers. Lots of things can be used as small containers. Make sure containers have drainage holes in the bottom to let water run out. Put saucers or trays underneath indoor pots so the water won't leak all over.

Soil for plants in pots. Plants in containers do best if you give them special soil that is airy enough to drain well and to let roots grow easily. You can buy bags of potting soil from any nursery or from many hardware stores, variety stores, or supermarkets.

If you have big containers that take lots of soil, you may be able to find places that sell potting soil in bulk (large amounts), which is usually cheaper. Check with places listed under "Topsoil" in the Yellow Pages of the phone book.

FIND A FLOWERPOT
You may already have something that you can use as a flowerpot. Try milk cartons cut in half, large plastic soft-drink bottles with the tops cut off, metal or plastic food containers. Just make sure there's enough room for your plant's roots to grow. Wash out containers well, and poke holes in the bottom for water to drain out.

Seeds in a container

Here's what you do when you plant seeds in containers.

1 Cover the drainage hole in the bottom of the container with a rock or a piece of a broken clay pot.

2 Fill the container with potting soil up to about an inch from the top.

3 Read the seed packet to see how deep your seeds should be planted. Poke holes that deep in the soil.

4 Put a seed in each hole. Press the soil lightly over the seed.

5 Water the soil gently with a fine spray. Wait a little bit and then water again the same way.

Keep the soil moist, but not soaking wet, while you are waiting for the seeds to sprout. After the plants have two pairs of leaves, pull out any plants that are too close together. The seed packet will tell you how far apart they should be.

Seedlings in a container

Leave enough space between seedlings in your container. A seed packet, a gardening book, or someone at a nursery can tell you how much. You can put flowers a little closer than the seed package says so that the pot will be filled with blossoms.

1 Cover the drainage hole in the bottom of the container with a rock or a piece of a broken clay pot.

2 Fill the container with potting soil up to about 2 inches from the top.

3 Water the soil. If it sinks down after you water it, add more soil so it comes to 2 inches from the top.

4 Carefully take the seedling out of its container and stretch out the roots a little bit.

5 Scoop out a hole and set the seedling in it, then press the soil gently around the plant to fill in the hole.

6 Water the soil until water begins to run out the drainage hole in the bottom.

A piece of broken pot keeps soil from coming out the drainage hole.

Bulbs in a container

There are two really easy ways to grow bulbs in containers—in soil or in water.

Bulbs grown in pots often won't bloom again the next year the way bulbs planted in the ground do. That's because they need more nutrients than the soil in one pot can give them. If you want to save your container bulbs, plant them in the ground after the flowers have dried, and they may bloom again. Keep watering until the leaves have dried up.

Planting bulbs in a pot of soil. You can plant one bulb in a small pot or lots of bulbs in a bigger pot. To make a bouquet in a container, set bulbs almost touching each other so that they fill up the pot.

1 Cover the drainage hole in the bottom of the container with a rock or a piece of a broken clay pot.

2 Partly fill the container with potting soil.

3 Mix bulb food into the soil. (Use as much as the directions say.) You can buy a bag of bulb food at the nursery.

4 Set the bulbs on the soil, right side up. Their tops shouldn't quite come to the top of the pot.

5 Cover the bulbs with potting soil.

6 Gently water the pot.

Daffodil bulbs

Set the pot outdoors and keep the soil moist but not soaking wet. When leaves start to show, put your container in a sunny spot. You can bring it indoors when the bulbs bloom, if you like.

Planting bulbs in water. Choose nice big hyacinth or paper-white narcissus bulbs. For each bulb, fill a glass with pea-size gravel or small rocks. (A 16-ounce plastic glass works well for a bulb to give as a present.) Gently push the bottom of the bulb into the gravel until it will stand by itself. Add water until the bottom inch of the bulb is covered.

Place the glass next to a sunny window and add water every so often to keep the bottom of the bulb wet. You'll be surprised how soon you have flowers.

Jar Jungles & Fishbowl Forests

WHAT YOU NEED

Glass container with an opening big enough for your hand—such as a cookie jar, a jar from a restaurant (1-gallon size or larger), a fishbowl, or an aquarium

Jar lid, plastic wrap (and a rubber band or string), or acrylic sheet (for an aquarium)

Aquarium gravel

Crushed charcoal

Potting soil

Old spoon with a long handle, or a narrow trowel

Plants

Spray bottle of water

Optional decorations such as ceramic or plastic animals, rocks, or marbles

A garden inside a jar—sometimes called a terrarium—is fun to make, pretty to look at, and fascinating to keep. You plant one or more plants in potting soil inside a large glass container, add water, and cover it up with a lid. Inside, your miniature garden becomes a little world with its own water supply.

The plants drink the water you put into your jar garden, then release it from their leaves as water vapor. The vapor collects as drops that run down the sides of the container into the soil, where they water the plants all over again.

How many plants you should choose depends on how big your container is and how you want it to look. You could plant just one, or a whole miniature jungle.

The aquarium gravel, crushed charcoal, and potting soil are all available from a nursery.

PLANTS FOR A JAR GARDEN

Choose small plants that won't grow too fast or too big. They should also be plants that like warm, moist air, like ferns or houseplants (especially ones with shiny leaves). Here are a few that work well:

Baby's tears (*Soleirolia*)

Dwarf dracaena

Maidenhair fern

Moss fern (*Selaginella*)

Nerve plant (*Fittonia*)

Peperomia

Prayer plant (*Maranta*)

Peace lily (*Spathiphyllum*)

1 Wash out your container with soap and hot water so it is very clean. Rinse it out several times, then dry it.

2 Using your spoon or trowel, scoop in a thin layer of gravel.

3 Add a thin layer of charcoal.

4 Now scoop in at least 3 inches of potting soil. Be sure to leave enough room above the soil for your plants to grow.

5 Use the spoon or spoon handle to make planting holes in the soil. Carefully remove your plants from their pots and loosen the soil around their roots. Place them in the planting holes and gently press the soil around them.

6 Carefully spray in a little water— not too much! The soil should be moist, not soggy.

7 Add any decorations you want.

8 Put on the lid or stretch plastic wrap over the top and fasten it with a rubber band or string.

Put your jar garden where it will get plenty of light but not *direct* sunlight, which will make it too hot. Watch it for a day or two. If the glass fogs up, take off the top for a few hours to let the garden "breathe." Then put the top back on.

Once your garden has the right amount of water, it won't need much care. If the soil looks dry, or if water doesn't drip down the sides anymore, open it and give it a little water. If the plants get too big, prune them carefully with scissors. Pick off dried or yellow leaves. Keep your jar garden healthy, and it may last a couple of years!

TAKING CARE OF YOUR PLANTS

Planting a garden is kind of like bringing a new pet into your house. It's exciting to pick out a kitten or puppy, but you can't just forget it once it's yours. You have to give it lots of care to make sure that it will be healthy and happy.

Plants are like that, too. It's fun to choose your plants and put them in the soil. But planting is just the beginning. Plants are living things that need your help to grow up strong. You have to take good care of them if you want them to be healthy in their new garden home.

Watering Your Garden

Some plants need lots of water. Others can get along without very much. Find out what your plants like by reading about them or asking at the nursery.

You can water with a watering can or a hose. If your watering can is big, fill it only partway so you can lift it. If you use a hose, adjust the nozzle to a fine spray to water seeds or seedlings. Otherwise you might blast them away.

You can also use a soaker attachment—a section of hose with little holes to let water drip out onto the ground. Or you can use a sprinkler attachment for your hose.

Here are some general tips about watering:

■ Poke your finger down into the soil. If it comes out dry, it's time to water.

■ Seeds and seedlings need watering often—they'll die if they dry out. Grown-up plants don't need water as often, but you need to give them enough each time so that it gets all the way down to their roots.

■ On hot, sunny days it is best to water outdoor plants in the early morning or early evening. This keeps water from drying up in the sun.

■ Water with lukewarm water, never ice-cold or hot water. If your hose has been lying in the sun, let the water run a few seconds until it doesn't feel hot.

■ Most plants don't like their roots to be soggy. Let the soil dry out partway before you water again.

■ Save water by spreading a layer of mulch over the soil. (Read about mulch on page 39.)

Getting water to the roots

You can help water get to your plants' roots. If you are growing plants in rows, dig shallow watering ditches, called "furrows," between rows. The furrows will hold the water so it can sink into the soil where the roots are growing.

For big plants growing by themselves, like tomato bushes or melon vines, you can make watering basins. Dig a little canal all around the plant. When you water, the water will run into this canal and sink into the soil right where the plant needs it.

Measuring the Rain

It's easy to measure how much rain falls in your garden. All you need is a simple rain gauge that you can make yourself. Here's how:

1 Hold a ruler straight up inside your container so that the end is touching the bottom, and use a waterproof pen to mark lines an inch apart on the outside. Write the numbers next to the lines.

2 Set your container outdoors in an open spot where there are no trees or roof edges above it and where it won't get knocked over. It should be level. It's a good idea to set it up off the ground on something flat, like a large flowerpot that's turned upside down. Or you can sink it into the ground a little bit to keep it from getting knocked over—just be sure it's level.

3 Every week, check to see how much rain is in the container. If you get less than 1 inch in a week, your garden probably needs watering! Dump out the water and start over for the next week.

WHAT YOU NEED

Straight-sided container that you can see through, such as an empty peanut butter jar

Ruler

Waterproof marking pen

Food for Plants

Plants get nutrients, or food, from the soil. Mixing compost or manure into your soil before you plant is one way to give your plants food. (Read how to do this on page 23.) But most plants also like an extra feeding now and then.

Food for plants is called "fertilizer." Fertilizers can be natural (organic) or chemical. Garden stores sell both kinds. Liquid fish emulsion and aged manure are two organic fertilizers. (They are smelly, but plants love them!) Chemical fertilizers come in both liquid and dry forms. Liquid plant food is usually the safest kind for kids to use.

A "complete" chemical fertilizer contains all three of the most important plant nutrients—nitrogen, phosphorus, and potassium. The most important of these is nitrogen, so you can look for the fertilizer with the most nitrogen at the cheapest price.

Feeding time

Some fertilizers need to be mixed with water. Otherwise they will be too strong and could harm your plants. Some kinds of dry fertilizers are mixed into the soil instead. Read the label and follow the directions for the kind you buy.

Once every 2 or 3 weeks should be often enough for most kinds of vegetables and flowers. Wear gloves when you use fertilizer, and keep fertilizer containers away from very young children.

MORE DIGGING!
One of the best ways to help your plants grow is to keep the soil around them cultivated. "Cultivate" means to dig in the soil to break up lumps, let air in, and keep weeds from growing. Cultivated soil warms up faster, too, and that makes plants grow faster. You can use a hand tool or a hoe to cultivate your soil—just don't get too close to plant roots. Try to do a little every time you work in your garden.

No Weeds Allowed!

A weed is any plant you don't want in your garden. If you let weeds grow, they'll steal food and water from the plants you do want.

The first rule of weeding is "Do it now!" Little weeds are a lot easier to get rid of than big ones. And they haven't had time to make seeds that will grow into more weeds.

Get the roots, or weeds will grow right back. If the soil is dry, water it to make it soft. Then grab the weed at the bottom of the stem and pull straight up. If a plant you want to keep starts to come out, too, press down on the soil around it with one hand as you pull up on the weed with the other hand.

A hand tool or a small shovel can help you get the tough ones. You can also chop out weeds with a hoe—but be careful not to chop any plants you are trying to grow.

Be sure to get the roots!

Mulch—a blanket for your garden

Weeding chores are a lot easier if you can keep weeds from growing in the first place. One way is to cover the soil around your plants with something called "mulch."

Mulch is anything you put down to keep sunlight from reaching the soil. That keeps weeds from growing, and it also keeps the soil from drying out so quickly. Sometimes mulch is also used to keep fruits or vegetables from getting dirty or rotting where they touch the ground. Compost, wood chips, and straw are some materials used as mulch. You can ask for suggestions at the nursery.

To use mulch, wait until after you have thinned your seedlings. Then spread out your mulch about 2 to 3 inches thick, without covering up your plants. If you use compost or another organic material as a mulch, you can dig it into the soil before the next growing season.

Garden Critters

If you have a garden, you also have a zoo! Many more animals than plants make their homes in your garden. Some of these animals are "good guys" that help your garden, but others are "bad guys" that will hurt your plants. Here's a guide to who's who in your zoo.

Garden good guys

These critters are all friendly to your garden—don't chase them away! Many of them eat insects that are harmful to your plants. Others help pollinate flowers or make the soil better.

Earthworms. Earthworms make tunnels that help water and air get deep into the soil, and that helps plants to grow. You can raise more worms for your garden—look on page 19.

Honeybees. When bees buzz around your flowers, the pollen that sticks to their legs gets carried to other plants. That helps plants make fruit or seeds.

Lacewings. These insects with the pretty wings make a meal of aphids and other harmful insects.

Ladybugs. The red beetles with the black spots on their backs eat lots and lots of aphids and other insect pests. So do the larvae—the baby bugs that will grow up to be ladybugs.

Spiders. You might not like spiders, but your garden will. Spiders trap many kinds of insects that could hurt your plants.

Toads, lizards, & birds. Toads and lizards help you out by eating caterpillars and insects that are unfriendly to plants. Many kinds of birds eat insects

Honeybee

Lacewing

Ladybug and ladybug larva

Toad

in a garden, too. (Birds may also like to dine on some of the fruits and vegetables you grow, so you may want to protect your crops with netting.)

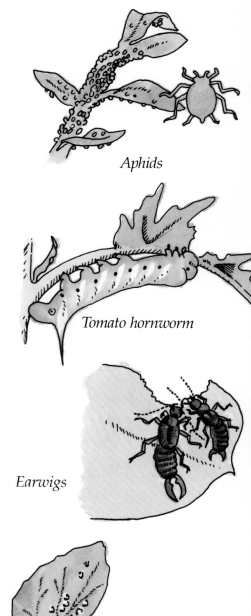
Aphids

Some bad guys

If you see leaves with holes or raggedy or curled edges, or stems that have been chewed in half, you know you have some unwanted garden visitors. Here are some of the "bad guys" that show up in gardens.

Aphids. Aphids suck the juices from plants, and that weakens and even kills plants. In one growing season, an aphid could start a family of 2 trillion more aphids! These tiny insects may be golden, black, or green.

Tomato hornworm

Caterpillars & worms. Cutworms, cabbage loopers, tomato hornworms, and other worms can do a lot of damage in a garden. Cutworms chew around a small plant so that it falls to the ground. Tomato hornworms and other worms can munch their way through a lot of leaves and vegetables.

Earwigs. Earwigs eat the soft parts of plants, such as flower petals.

Earwigs

Snails & slugs. Snails and slugs come out at night or on damp, gray days to eat leaves and flowers. They slide over the ground on a trail of silvery slime, and they can gobble up a whole seedling overnight.

Whiteflies. These tiny insects suck plant juices, and that takes away energy that plants need to grow.

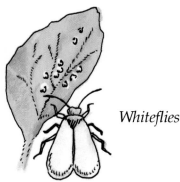
Whiteflies

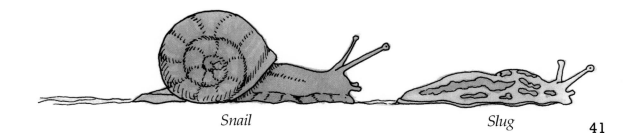
Snail   Slug

41

Getting rid of the bad guys

Only a few of the critters in your garden are harmful. Using poisons to get rid of the bad guys can hurt the good guys, too. It's not safe for you, either. Here are some safer ways to control the critters you don't want around.

■ Blast aphids or whiteflies with a spray of water from a hose.

■ Protect a seedling from cutworms by putting a kind of wall or collar around it. Part of a milk carton works well.

■ Make an earwig trap by rolling up a damp newspaper and leaving it in the garden overnight. In the morning, put the trap (and the earwigs that have crawled inside) into a plastic bag and throw it in the garbage can.

■ Stomp on snails or squash them with a trowel and then bury them or put them in a plastic bag to throw away.

■ Make a trap for snails and slugs by raising a board a little off the ground. Collect the snails and slugs that hide there during the day.

■ Pick off big worms by hand. (Wear gloves if you don't like to touch them.)

■ Spray soapy water on aphids, whiteflies, and other small insect pests. You can buy insect soap sprays or make your own. Mix 1 tablespoon of liquid dishwashing soap (not detergent) with 1 quart of water. An hour or so after you spray the soapy water on a plant, rinse it off with plain water.

You will probably have to put up with some pests in your garden, but don't worry too much about it. If they are a real problem, you can go to the garden store and ask for an organic pesticide. Have an adult help you use it.

WHO LIVES HERE?
If you spent an afternoon digging through a 3-foot-square area on the ground, you'd meet more than 2,000 insects! You would need a microscope to see some of them—they are too tiny to see with just your eyes.

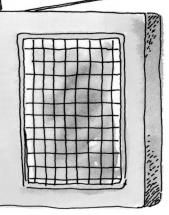

WEATHER WATCH
You can find out when your plants might need to be protected from the weather. Listen to the weather report on the radio or television, or read the weather report in a newspaper.

Weatherwise

When the weather turns extra cold or extra hot, you know what to do to keep yourself comfortable. Your outdoor plants need the same kind of care.

Brrrr! It's cold!

On really cold nights, bring potted plants that don't like the cold indoors if you can. Plants in pots will also stay warmer if you put them in a garage, on a covered porch, or even under a tree.

If a plant is in the ground, you can make an overnight shelter for it. Push some sticks or stakes into the ground around the plant. Then cover the sticks with a large plastic bag or an old sheet. Don't let the bag or sheet touch the plant. Take the covering off in the morning.

Whew! It's hot!

On really hot summer days, make sure your plants have enough water to drink. Move potted plants into the shade if you can.

To protect a small plant growing in the ground, you can make a tent to shade it from the hot sun. Fold a few sheets of newspaper together and set them up in a tent shape over the plant. Hold down the edges with rocks or dirt. Remember to take away the tent when the weather gets cooler.

Tidying Up

Your room often needs tidying up. So do your plants! They will look nicer—and may grow better—if you do these things.

Removing faded flowers

Flowers look prettier and often produce more blossoms if you do something with kind of a weird name—"deadheading." Deadheading means cutting or pinching off any blossoms that have faded and started to dry. Then the plant can use its energy to make more flowers.

Pinching

Tall and skinny or short and bushy—that's your choice. You can help a plant to grow either way by pinching off growth buds.

Plants grow in two directions, upward and sideways. If you want a bushier plant, use your thumb and finger to pinch off new buds at the top of the plant. That way the plant will grow sideways instead. To make a taller plant, pinch off new buds at the side of the plant. The plant will grow up.

Pruning

Sometimes a plant grows a little too big, gets a little too bushy, or has a dead branch. You can make the plant look better and grow healthier by pruning it—cutting off the part you don't want or don't need. Use scissors, or get help from an adult to use pruning shears.

Supports for Plants

If you plant bushy vegetables, very tall flowers, or plants that like to climb, they may need some help standing up.

Plants in cages. A cage for a tomato plant? No, your plant won't run away without one, but a cage will help hold up a bushy plant. A cage is a little fence that goes around the plant. You can get one at a garden store or ask an adult to help you make one. A tomato plant in a cage takes up less room, too.

Staking. Tall flowers sometimes need support to keep the wind from blowing them over. Poke a long stick or a stake from the garden store into the ground next to the flower. Carefully tie thick yarn, a strip of cloth, or a soft plastic plant tie around the stick and the stem. Don't pull it tight—your plant needs room to grow.

Trellises. Vining plants such as peas need something to climb on. You can buy trellises, or you can ask an adult to help you make one. When your vines start to grow, help them find the trellis strings.

If you have a wooden fence, you can pound nails partway into the wood at the top and bottom of the fence. Tie string to the first nail on the top, pull it down to the first bottom nail and across to the second bottom nail, stretch it back up to the second top nail, and so on until it winds up and down all along the fence.

Here is kind of trellis you can move. Nail together 1-by-1 or 2-by-2 pieces of wood to make two frames 4 to 6 feet on each side. Fasten the frames together at the top with hinges so that you can set them up to make an A-frame. Then pound nails into the top and bottom edge of each frame and pull string up and down in straight lines around the nails.

Twisting a plant tie into a figure-8 helps hold it in place.

A HINT FOR TOMATO PICKERS
Tomatoes sold in stores usually are picked when they are green. That's so they won't get squashed during shipping. Homegrown tomatoes can stay on the vine until they turn ripe and juicy. Pick your tomatoes when they are bright red. Yum!

Harvest Time

After all the work and waiting, it's finally time to pick what you have grown! Put your senses to work to decide if your fruits and vegetables are ready to pick. Does the fruit or vegetable *look* ripe? Does it *smell* ripe? And does it *taste* ripe?

How to pick

Be gentle when you pick your fruits and vegetables. You don't want to hurt the plants. Use one hand to pick and the other to hold the plant.

You'll need a knife, pruning shears, or scissors to cut flowers. Ask a grown-up for help if you need it.

Storing what you pick

Fruits and vegetables usually taste their very best if you eat them soon after you pick them. Store them in the refrigerator to keep them fresh tasting.

Freezing, canning, and drying are ways to keep foods longer. Books in the library can tell you about these ways of storing foods.

Sharing your crops

Part of the fun of growing food is sharing it. If you have too many fruits or vegetables for your family to use, take some to friends and neighbors.

In many towns and cities, your extra food is welcome at places that serve meals to people who need help.

Bouquets to bring indoors

A bouquet of flowers from your garden can make the family dinner table special. Here's how to make your cut flowers stay beautiful longer.

Flowers last longest if you cut them in the morning and choose buds that are just starting to open. Cut as long a stem as you can without cutting off any buds that you want to open later.

Pull off all the leaves that will be under water in the vase. Then put the stems in fresh water in your container right away. Change the water every day or two to keep it fresh.

At Season's End

Most good things come to an end. That's true for many of the plants in your garden, too. Here's what to do when the growing season is over.

Flowers that are annuals

Annuals live and die in one growing season. They won't bloom again, so the compost pile or trash can is the place for them when the season is over.

Flowers that are perennials

Perennials can live for many years. To put them to bed for the winter, ask an adult to help you cut them down to the ground. (You can put the parts you cut off in the compost pile.) Then tuck the plants in under a layer of mulch, such as ground-up bark or sawdust. The roots will make new plants again the next growing season.

Flowers that grow from bulbs

Flowers that grow from bulbs, such as tulips and daffodils, need to get their energy back after they finish blooming. Even though their leaves look a little messy, don't pull them off until they are yellow and soft. They are making food for next year's flowers.

The vegetable garden

When your tomatoes, corn, and other vegetables are finished for the season, you can pull out the leftover parts and use them in a compost pile. (Chop or tear the plants into small pieces first.)

Keeping the weeds away

A bare garden plot is a great place for weeds to start growing. A mulch blanket is one way to keep weeds from taking over while your garden is resting.

Cover the garden area with a layer of mulch about 4 inches deep. This will keep most weeds from growing. In the spring, you can dig organic mulches such as compost or leaf mold into the soil to help your new plants grow. (Read more about mulch on page 39.)

SHHH! GARDEN SLEEPING

Painting with Plants

Did you know that you can paint with the plants in your garden? The leaves of just about any plant make wonderful designs when you "paint" with them on paper. And a potato or turnip from your garden (or from the supermarket) can be carved to make your own printing stamp. The paper you decorate can be used for almost anything, from wrapping paper to recipe cards.

How to do it

Cover your work surface with several layers of newspaper and lay out your supplies, including a piece of paper to practice on. Pour a little paint into your trays. It's best to use a separate tray for each color, but you can put two colors in a large tray if you are careful to keep them from running together. Clean your brush whenever you change colors.

Making a leaf print. Most leaves can be used over again several times during a printing session. Wash them off if you change colors.

1 Lay your leaf, smooth side up, on the newspapers. Hold it down by the stem and brush paint all over it.

2 Carefully lift up your leaf by the stem and lay it on your printing paper, painted side down.

3 Put a piece of paper towel on top of the leaf, then use your soup can like a little rolling pin to roll gently but firmly over the leaf and towel.

4 Carefully lift off the paper towel, then the leaf. There's your painting!

WHAT YOU NEED

Old newspapers

Poster paints

Plastic food trays, aluminum foil pie plates, or other containers

Paintbrush

White or colored paper to print on (paper that's not too slick works best)

Paper towels for cleanup

For leaf prints:

Leaves from different kinds of plants

Clean paper towels

Empty soup can or smooth-sided jar

For potato prints:

Large raw potato or turnip, unpeeled

Small, sharp-pointed knife

Small cookie cutters

Printing with a potato. If you want to use your potato printer again within a few days, rinse it off and dry it. Then wrap it or put it in an airtight container and save it in the refrigerator.

1 Get an adult to help you slice your potato in half. (Slicing it lengthwise may give you more surface to work with.)

2 Push a cookie cutter into the cut side of the potato so that the cookie cutter edge is about halfway in.

3 With adult help, use the point of your knife to cut away the potato all around the cookie cutter. Carefully pull out the cookie cutter.

4 Brush paint onto the raised design.

5 Press the potato stamp down on the paper. Lift it straight up to take it off the paper without smearing.

If you want to make your own design instead of using a cookie cutter, draw it on the potato with a felt-tip pen. Cut away the potato all around the design.

With a potato or some leaves, you can print your own wrapping paper, stationery, gift tags—or whatever you can think up.

Plants in Containers

A plant in a pot has the same needs as a plant in the ground. But a potted plant depends on you even more than its cousins in the ground do. On these pages, you can learn about taking care of your plants in containers.

A potted plant needs water

In the ground, a plant can send roots down deep to find water. But in a pot, a plant has only a small amount of soil in which to grow. When the soil in its pot is dry, a potted plant is out of luck unless you help.

Test to see if the soil is dry by poking your finger into it. An outdoor potted plant may need water every day. For indoor plants, start by watering once a week. Try to do it on the same day of the week so you won't forget. Then watch the plant. If it starts to droop or the soil is very dry when you touch it, try watering every 5 days instead of every week. Don't water too often—that will kill a houseplant fast.

Ways to water. A watering can is a good way to water your plants in pots. For outdoor plants, use a sprinkler attachment on the watering can—the water will pour out gently, almost like rain. For indoor plants, a watering can with a long, thin spout makes it easier to keep from spilling.

SAVE SOME WATER
Some people save the water that runs out of a faucet while they are waiting for it to get hot enough to take a shower or wash dishes. They use that saved water for their plants.

A long spout makes it easy to give a piggyback plant a drink of water.

A garden hose is another way to water your outdoor plants. Turn the hose on low. If you use a strong spray, it will wash soil out of the pot. Then you'll have a muddy mess, and your plant will have less soil in which to grow. If you use a hose on a hot day, let the water run a few seconds until it feels cool.

You can also use a bucket and a cup to water your plants in containers.

How much water? Keep watering until some water runs out of the drainage holes in the bottom of the pot. If you are watering an indoor plant, use a saucer to catch the extra water. Empty the water from the saucer—plants don't like their "feet" to stay wet.

Some plants may need to be watered from the bottom.

Another way to water. Sometimes a plant's roots fill up so much of the pot that they can't get enough water from the top. It just runs out of the pot before the roots can get a good drink. Here's how to water these plants.

Set the pot in a pan, bowl, or bucket. Pour water into the pan until it comes partway up the side of the pot. Then just wait awhile. The plant will drink the water from the bottom. When the soil at the top of the pot is wet, you know it has had enough.

Vacation watering. If you go away for a few days, ask a friend or neighbor to water your plants. Another way to keep your plants watered is to make a self-watering system. You need a wide pan, like a dishpan, and some nylon cord wicks from a nursery. Fill the pan with water and set your plants around it. Cut a piece of cord for each plant. Soak the cords in water and then push one end of a cord 1 or 2 inches into the soil in each pot. Put the other end into the water. Water will go through the wicks to your plants.

A potted plant needs food

A plant in a container can quickly use up the food in its soil. Then the plant depends on you to feed it. About every 2 to 4 weeks, add some liquid fertilizer from the plant store to your watering can. Read the directions on the label and follow them carefully. Too much plant food at one time can hurt your plant.

Another way to feed plants in pots is to buy little fertilizer stakes or tablets that you stick into the soil. They last a long time.

Remember to feed your potted plants, like this coleus.

Goodbye to weeds

One big advantage of a potted plant is that it doesn't usually need to be weeded. However, weed seeds can blow into a pot or be carried by birds or animals. If a weed starts to grow, pull it out. It can steal water and food from your plant.

Protection from critters

Insects and other critters can hurt a potted plant. Read about how to control those pests on page 42.

Keeping your potted plants clean helps keep them healthy. Houseplants with leaves that are shiny (not fuzzy) can be wiped off with a cloth dampened with warm water to keep them clean.

Tidying up

Your potted plant is probably in a place where you look at it often, so you'll want to keep it tidy. Pick off the dead leaves and flowers. Then your plant will look better and grow better, too. To make your plant grow in the shape you want, pinch off buds as explained on page 44.

A container garden can look pretty all year. If plants have finished blooming or need a rest, you can move them to another spot. Replace them with plants that look their best.

When plants outgrow their pots

Sometimes a plant gets too big for its pot. If a plant is so big that the pot tips over, or if it dries out quickly because its roots are too crowded, it's time to move it to a new pot. This is called "transplanting."

You can check to see if the roots are too crowded by taking the plant out of its pot. Run an old table knife around the inside of the pot, hold the pot upside down, and tap the bottom. Put one hand around the plant to keep it from falling when it slides out. Now look at the roots. Are they growing up to the top of the pot? Are they all matted together? If they are, it's time to move to a pot that's just a little bit bigger.

Gently pull apart the tangled-up roots with your fingers, or have a grown-up helper use a sharp knife to make ½-inch-deep slices in the bottom and sides of the root ball. Now move your plant into moist potting soil in its new container. Gently water it.

A SONG FOR YOUR PLANT
Will your plant grow better if you sing to it? There are people who think so! Some people play soft music for their plants, too. Try it just for fun.

A Christmas Tree to Keep

Wouldn't it be fun to have a little Christmas tree to decorate just the way you want? You can get a small live tree in a container to bring inside at Christmas, then keep outdoors the rest of the year. If you take good care of it, you'll be able to keep it for years.

Garden stores usually have lots of small live Christmas trees during the holiday season. Your job is to pick out a small but healthy-looking tree that will grow slowly, so it won't get too big for its pot too soon. One good choice is a dwarf Alberta spruce in a 1-gallon container. Ask at the nursery for more suggestions. Some other kinds you may find are alpine fir, noble fir, Black Hills spruce, and Colorado spruce.

Indoors & outdoors

If you live where winter is very cold, put your tree on a porch or next to a window in an unheated garage or basement for a couple of days before you bring it indoors. This helps it get used to the change in temperature. In any climate, water your tree well the day before you bring it in.

Place your tree away from heaters or direct sunshine, and water it every 2 or 3 days while it's indoors. Use a saucer under the tree to catch drips.

It's best not to keep a live tree indoors longer than 10 days. When the holidays are over, put it outdoors where it's protected from wind and hot afternoon sun. If you live in a cold-winter climate, get it used to the temperature change the same way you did when you brought it inside.

Water your tree outdoors every week, or more if the soil dries out. You can fertilize it once in the spring and once in the summer. (Find out how on page 52.)

Dwarf Alberta spruce

MAKING MORE PLANTS

Recycling is not just for cans and bottles. You can recycle plants, too. You can turn the seeds, stems, and leaves of many plants into brand-new plants. It doesn't cost you anything—and it's fun!

This chapter will show you several ways to make more plants from those you already have. With your new plant "babies," you might want to set up a plant trading post with your friends. Plants you have started yourself also make good presents.

Sunflower

Collecting & Storing Seeds

Garden stores sell seeds in little paper packages. But seeds come in other kinds of packages, too. Flowers, fruit, and pine cones are all natural seed packages. You can collect seeds from some of these packages to use next planting season.

Sometimes the seeds that come from these natural packages will surprise you. The plants that grow from them may not look just like the plants that gave you the seeds in the first place! If you want to be absolutely sure of what you're getting, buy your seeds from the garden store. If you don't care, you can have fun seeing what comes up when you plant the seeds you've collected yourself.

Seeds from flowers

When most flowers finish blooming, they "go to seed." That means that their flowers dry up and start to form seeds. Here's one way to collect these seeds to grow more flowers:

1 Tie a bag over a blossom that has dried up.

2 Wait for seeds to fall into the bag. (It may take a few days. You can help things along by giving the bag a little shake.)

3 Use scissors to cut the blossom, with the bag attached, off the plant.

4 Carefully open the bag and remove the seeds. Save them in an envelope that you have marked with the name of the flower.

5 Keep the seeds in a dry place indoors, away from heat, until it is time for planting. It's best to use your seeds within a year's time.

Seeds from fruits & vegetables

For fun, you can also collect seeds from fruits and vegetables, but the plants you grow from these seeds may turn out to be different from what you expect. They may not produce fruit or vegetables that you can eat.

But you can experiment, anyway. A watermelon is pretty easy to try. Pick out the biggest and blackest seeds from a ripe watermelon, let them dry out completely, and store them until it is planting time.

Seeds from trees

Pine cones are the seed packages for pine trees. You can grow some kinds of pine trees by collecting the seeds from their cones. If you want to try, choose a brown cone that hasn't opened up yet, and pull it off the tree. Put it in a paper bag and keep it someplace warm (such as near a water heater or oven) for several days until the pine cone opens up and its seeds fall out. Store the seeds in a dry place indoors, away from heat, until you are ready to plant them.

You can also plant acorns to start baby oak trees. Collect a few acorns from a tree and put them in a bowl or bucket of water. The healthy acorns will sink to the bottom—plant them in a pot and then transplant the seedlings into the ground. (If you put acorns right in the ground, gophers might eat the nuts before they can sprout.)

Another easy tree seed to start is a maple. The seed looks like a little helicopter.

FLOWERS FOR SEED COLLECTING

It's easier to collect seeds from some kinds of flowers than others. Here are some good ones to try.

African daisy	Hollyhock
Calendula	Marigold
California poppy	Nasturtium
Cornflower	Sunflower
Cosmos	Sweet pea
Four o'clock	Zinnia

New Plants from Stem Cuttings

Snip! With just the snip of a scissors, you can be on your way to starting a new plant. All you need to do is make a cutting—a piece of stem or a leaf that you cut off a plant. Then you can watch the cutting grow into a brand-new plant.

Here are some especially easy plants to start from stem cuttings:

Begonia   **Grape ivy**

Coleus   **Impatiens**

Geranium   **Philodendron**

Many other plants will work, too. After you have tried one of the easy-to-start cuttings, experiment with your own favorite plants.

Here's how to take a stem cutting from a plant:

1 Choose a stem 4 or 5 inches long.

2 With scissors, cut off the stem through the base of a leaf, as shown below. (You may need help from an adult.)

3 Pinch off the leaves on the bottom half of your cutting.

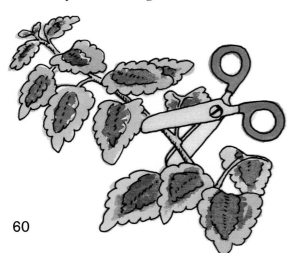

Now you are ready to help your stem cutting start to grow. You can put it either in soil or in water. If you make two cuttings from a plant, you can find out which way is faster.

Starting a stem cutting in water
You need a glass or a bottle filled with lukewarm water.

1 Put the end of the cutting in the glass of water, keeping the leaves above the water.

2 Watch for a new root to grow from the stem. (It may take several weeks.) When roots are 3 or 4 inches long, you can move your cutting into a pot.

Starting a stem cutting in soil

To start your cutting growing in soil, you will need a small pot, a package of rooting powder from the garden store, and some potting soil (the kind you buy in bags).

1 Dip the end of the stem cutting in the rooting powder. (This helps roots grow faster.)

2 Cover the drainage hole in your pot with a rock or a piece of a broken pot. Fill the pot with potting soil to about an inch from the top.

3 With your finger, poke a hole about 2 inches deep in the soil.

4 Carefully stick the cutting down into the hole, and then lightly press the soil around it to fill up the hole.

5 Add a little water to moisten the soil.

6 Put the plant in a bright, warm spot, out of direct sunlight, and watch for it to grow. (It will probably take several weeks.) Keep watering it to keep the soil moist.

Here's how to tell when a root has grown from your cutting. After about 3 or 4 weeks, pull very gently on the cutting. If it doesn't come out of the soil, a root is holding it in. Soon you should also start to see some new little leaves on your cutting. When the new plant gets too big for its pot, you can move it into a bigger container.

THIS LITTLE PIGGY...

A kind of houseplant called a piggyback plant grows new leaves right out of the old leaves—piggyback style! To start a new piggyback plant, cut off a leaf that has a baby leaf attached. Stick it in moist potting soil so that the bottom of the leaf touches the soil.

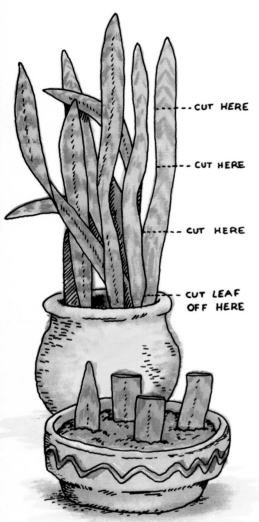

CUT HERE

CUT HERE

CUT HERE

CUT LEAF
OFF HERE

A New Plant from a Leaf

Some new plants will grow right from the leaves of plants. One that is fun and easy to try is a snake plant, which has long, snaky leaves that stick straight up. Another name for this plant is sansevieria.

1 Cover the drainage hole in the bottom of a pot with a rock or a piece of a broken pot. Then fill the pot with potting soil to about an inch from the top. Water the soil so that it is moist.

2 Cut one of the long leaves from the snake plant, using scissors. (You may need an adult helper.)

3 Cut the leaf crosswise into four pieces.

4 Stick each piece, bottom edge down, partway into the potting soil.

5 Watch for new plants to grow along the bottom edges of the leaf pieces. Water as often as you need to so that the soil stays moist.

Layering to Grow Baby Spiders

Layering isn't just a way to keep warm by piling on sweaters and jackets. It's also a way to start a new plant. In layering, the new plant is started while it is still attached to its "mother" plant. A good plant to try this with is a spider plant. (You can read more about spider plants on page 93.)

A spider plant has baby leaves that look a little like spiders. You can put one of these spider plant babies in a pot of its own to grow into a separate plant with its own roots. Here's how:

1 Put a rock or a piece of a broken pot over the drainage hole in the bottom of a pot. Then fill the pot with potting soil to about an inch from the top. Water the soil so that it is moist.

2 Set the pot next to a large spider plant and then set a spider "baby" from the plant on the potting soil in the pot. Don't cut the two plants apart yet.

3 Bend a piece of wire into a "U" shape and carefully poke the ends into the potting soil to hold the baby in place. (A straightened-out paper clip works well.)

4 Keep watering so that the soil stays moist while the new plant is growing.

5 After the baby has grown its own roots, use scissors to cut off the part that connects it to its "mother." Now you have two plants instead of one!

A Recycled Garden

Stop! Don't take those kitchen scraps to the compost heap yet. You may have enough treasures to start a special garden—a garden from kitchen leftovers.

A Curly-top Carrot

WHAT YOU NEED

Carrot with its green top removed (or a turnip, beet, or parsnip)

Sharp knife

Plate or shallow dish

The tops of carrots can grow into a miniature jungle. And you can eat the part of the carrot you don't use!

1 Cut the top 1 inch off the carrot. (Be sure to ask for adult help if you need it.)

2 Put the carrot top on the plate, cut side down.

3 Add just enough water to make the bottom of the carrot wet.

4 Put the plate next to a sunny window.

5 Water the carrot a little bit every day so that the bottom stays wet.

Now watch for leaves to grow out of the top. If you want to give your carrot some company, do the same thing with a turnip, a beet, or a parsnip.

Carrots and a turnip

WHAT YOU NEED

3 seeds from an orange
Small pot
A rock or a piece of
    a broken pot
Potting soil

A Baby Orange Tree

You may not ever get oranges from this tree, but you'll have fun watching it grow.

1 Put a rock or a piece of a broken pot over the drainage hole in your pot. Then fill the pot almost to the top with potting soil.

2 Water the soil just enough to make it moist.

3 Poke three holes 1 to 2 inches deep in the potting soil and put a seed in each hole. Fill in the holes with potting soil.

4 Gently water the seeds.

Put the pot in a sunny window. Water the seeds a little every day—don't let the soil dry out! After leaves have grown, be sure to keep watering regularly.

An Avocado Tree

The avocado tree you grow from a seed may not give you any avocados, but it will look nice.

1 Wash off the avocado seed and let it dry for two days.

2 Push the toothpicks into the seed, evenly spaced around its middle.

3 Balance the toothpicks on the glass so that the pointed end of the avocado seed is on top.

4 Pour enough water into the glass to cover the bottom half of the seed.

Check every day to see if you need to add water. In a month or so, you should see a root. When the root is about 5 inches long, remove the seed from the glass and take out the toothpicks. Then you can plant it in potting soil in a pot. Leave about 1 inch of the seed sticking out of the soil. Put the pot in a sunny window and keep it watered.

WHAT YOU NEED

Avocado seed
4 toothpicks
Glass or jar about
    6 inches tall

FUN PLANTS TO GROW

As a gardener, you will learn how amazingly different one plant is from another. No two leaves are exactly the same shape. No two flowers have exactly the same color or smell.

This chapter will introduce you to lots of interesting and beautiful plants that you can grow and compare. Some of them are good to eat, and others have pretty flowers or leaves. Read through and see what looks good to you. Grow one plant in a pot, or grow 50 flowers in the garden—either way, you'll have lots of fun.

The plants described in this chapter are all good choices for kids' gardens. But there are lots and lots of other plants you can grow, too. If something at the nursery or in a catalog appeals to you, just check to see if your garden has the right sun and weather conditions. Then give it a try.

Nicknames for plants

Plants have both a common name and a scientific name—just like some kids have both a nickname and a real name. Common names, like "sunflower" or "squash," are like nicknames. Sometimes two different plants have the same nickname. Or one plant may have more than one nickname! This can make it confusing when you shop for a particular plant.

Scientific names end the confusion, because no two plants can have the same scientific name. Even though they may sound like tongue twisters, scientific names can help you find exactly the plant you are looking for.

In this book, only the common name is given for most plants. But if a plant could be confused with another plant, we also tell you the scientific name. Show it to someone at the garden store so you can be sure you get the plant you want.

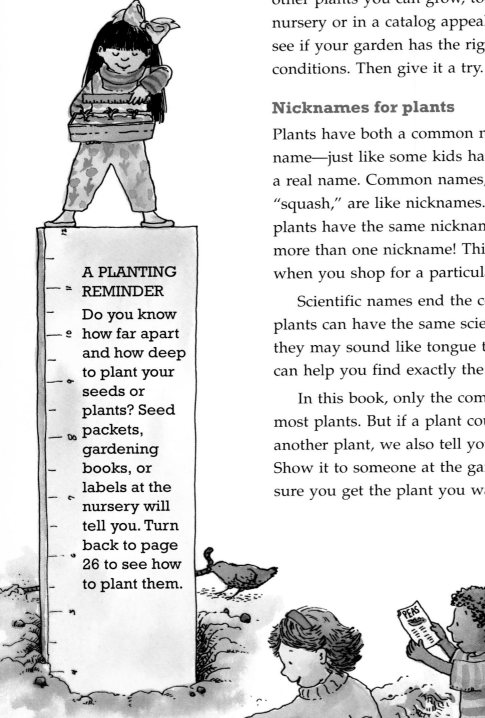

A PLANTING REMINDER

Do you know how far apart and how deep to plant your seeds or plants? Seed packets, gardening books, or labels at the nursery will tell you. Turn back to page 26 to see how to plant them.

Vegetables & Fruits

Nothing tastes better than vegetables and fruits from your own garden. Picked just when they're ripe, homegrown can taste so much better than store-bought that you'll have a hard time believing they are the same thing.

When to plant them

Some vegetables and fruits grow best in cool soil and can live through a light frost (like lettuce). Some grow best in warm soil and will be killed by a light frost (like tomatoes).

Vegetables that like cool soil are usually planted in early spring, several weeks *before* the average last spring frost date. That way they are all grown before the heat of summer. Many cool-loving vegetables can also be planted in late summer to ripen in the fall.

Vegetables that like warm soil are usually planted *after* the last spring frost date. That way they can grow in the heat of summer, just the way they like it.

In areas with long, cold winters and short summers, you can plant many cool-loving vegetables all summer. To grow warm-loving vegetables in these areas, choose early maturing varieties. They'll be marked "early" in seed catalogs.

To find out the frost date where you live, read page 18.

Where to plant them

Choose the sunniest place possible. Some vegetables—especially if we eat the leaves or roots—can grow in a little bit of shade, but even these grow best with at least 6 hours a day of direct sunlight.

Many vegetables and some fruits can be grown in containers. Usually, the bigger the pot the better. Half-barrels work great. Lettuce, carrots, and radishes can be grown in small pots. Read about each plant in the next few pages to find out whether or not it can be grown in a container. Even if it can, it still needs to be outdoors to get enough sunlight.

How to grow them

Some vegetables grow best if you start with seeds. Others are best to start from seedlings. You can grow your own seedlings indoors if you like—see page 25.

All vegetables and fruits need good soil, and regular water and fertilizer. Read page 23 to see how to add organic matter, such as compost or manure, to the soil. Fertilize most vegetables every 2 or 3 weeks (see page 38). A few kinds need fertilizer even more often.

After your seeds sprout, pull out any seedlings that are too close together. Crowded vegetables probably won't grow right.

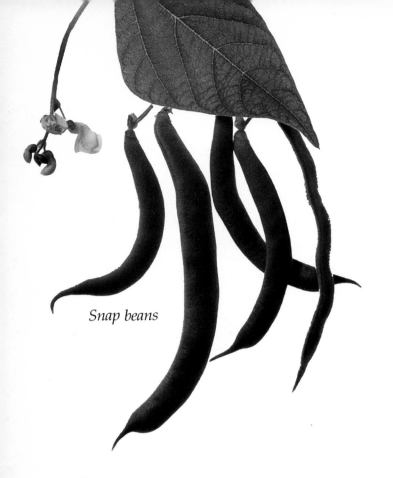

Snap beans

Beans

There are a lot of different kinds of beans, but all of them are either pole beans or bush beans. Pole beans grow on climbing vines and need a fence or trellis to hold them up (see page 45). Bush beans grow on short plants that don't need a trellis, so they are easiest to grow.

Beans are also either "snap" or "shell" beans. Snap beans are the kind you eat when they are soft and tender, pod and all. Shell beans (such as lima beans) are usually allowed to dry on the plant. Then you remove the shell and just cook the beans that are inside.

When to plant. After the last spring frost. You can keep planting until the middle of summer.

How to plant. Plant bean seeds 1½ to 2 inches deep. Be sure pole beans are next to a fence or trellis. Seeds will sprout in 6 to 14 days. Thin bush bean seedlings to 2 to 3 inches apart, pole beans to 4 to 6 inches apart.

Grow in containers? You can grow bush beans in large containers.

When to harvest. You can usually begin picking 1½ to 2 months after planting. Pick snap beans when they are about 3 to 5 inches long. If you leave them on the plant too long, they'll get tough and stringy. The more you pick, the more the plant will make all during the growing season. Pick shell beans when they have dried but before the pod splits open.

Carrots

Wait until you taste fresh carrots from the garden! You won't believe how sweet they are—especially the short varieties. Preparing the soil well and thinning seedlings are very important steps toward getting a good carrot crop.

When to plant. You'll get best results by starting about 6 weeks before the last frost date, but you can keep planting at least until mid-spring in most areas. You can also plant carrots in late summer for a fall and winter crop.

How to plant. Scatter the tiny seeds, or plant in rows. Just barely cover the seeds with about ¼ inch of soil. Germination usually takes 10 to 17 days. Thin the seedlings so they are 1 to 2 inches apart.

Grow in containers? Yes. Short varieties are best. Use a pot at least 12 inches deep.

When to harvest. Carrots take 2 to 3 months to reach full size, but you can start picking them sooner—when they get to be about half an inch thick. Pull one out to see if they're ready.

Corn

You need a lot of room to grow corn. The plants can reach more than 8 feet high, and each one only makes 2 or 3 ears of corn, so you have to plant enough for several meals. You also have to plant at least 3 rows so that enough pollen from tassels on top of the plant falls down onto the corn silk (the hairy ends of the ears of corn). Otherwise, the corn kernels won't develop properly.

When to plant. After the last spring frost. You can keep planting until the middle of summer.

How to plant. Plant seeds 2 inches deep, with 30 to 36 inches between rows. In 6 to 10 days you should see seedlings. Thin the seedlings to 10 to 14 inches apart.

Grow in containers? No, corn needs more room to grow properly.

When to harvest. Corn takes 2 to 3 months from seed to harvest. You have to pick the ears as soon as they are ready, or they start going bad in a few days. When the corn silk starts to dry, gently pull back the leaves around the ear and look at the kernels. They should be rounded and have nice color. Stick your fingernail in a kernel. If milky white juice spurts out, it is ready. By the way, if you find a small worm at the end of an ear, don't worry—he just took a taste. Have a grown-up cut off that part.

Carrot

Corn

Lettuce

You'll be surprised how many different lettuce colors and leaf shapes there are. Start with leaf lettuce, since it's easier to grow than head lettuce.

When to plant. You can plant in early spring 6 to 8 weeks before the last frost and continue into mid-spring, whether you are planting seeds or seedlings. Or start in late summer for a fall crop.

How to plant. You can plant either seeds or seedlings. Just barely cover seeds with about ¼ inch of soil. Wait 4 to 10 days for your first sprouts. Thin seedlings so there are 4 to 6 inches between plants.

Grow in containers? Lettuce grows and looks great in any pot that is at least 6 inches wide.

When to harvest. Lettuce usually takes 1½ to 2 months to fully mature, but you can start picking as soon as you think you have enough for a salad. You can pull the whole plant or pick just the outer leaves, which lets the plant keep growing and giving you more leaves.

Leaf lettuce

Melons

What could taste better on a hot summer day than sweet and juicy watermelon or cantaloupe? Most melons need lots of room, summers that are long and hot, and plenty of water and fertilizer. Small round "icebox" varieties are usually the most convenient watermelons to grow.

When to plant. In warm soil, usually 2 to 3 weeks after the last spring frost.

How to plant. Push soil up into circular mounds 1 to 2 feet wide. Leave 4 to 6 feet between mounds if you have more than one. Flatten the top of the mound with your hand, and scoop out a watering basin all around the mound, like a moat around a sand castle.

Plant 3 or 4 seeds, about 1 inch deep, in the top of each mound. Space them about 10 to 12 inches apart. Seeds usually sprout in 3 to 12 days.

Grow in containers? Some bush varieties of cantaloupe, such as

Melon planting mound

Peas

Peas grow on vines that can climb up to 6 feet high. They will grow best if they are supported by a wire fence or a trellis. There are two types of peas—snap peas, which you eat pod and all, and regular garden peas, which are shelled to eat.

When to plant. Peas like a long, cool growing season, so start as early in spring as possible—as soon as the ground can be dug. In the South and West where the climate is mild, you can also plant in late summer or early fall.

How to plant. Plant seeds 2 inches deep next to a trellis or fence. (See page 45 for an easy trellis to make.) Sprouts will appear in 6 to 15 days. Thin the seedlings to 2 to 3 inches apart. You don't need to fasten the peas to the trellis, but you can help the curly tendrils find the strings to climb on.

Grow in containers? It's better to plant peas in the ground.

When to harvest. Peas usually take about 2 to 2½ months from seed to harvest. Pick snap peas early—when they reach 2 to 3 inches long and when you can just start to see the peas growing in the pod. Pick garden peas when the pods have swelled to almost round shape. Pick both kinds of peas often so that they don't get tough.

'Honeybush', can be grown in large pots. Small bush varieties of watermelon could be grown in a container, but all melons really do best in the ground.

When to harvest. Watermelons and cantaloupes usually take 2½ to 3½ months from seed to picking time. To tell if a watermelon is ripe, knock on it with your knuckles, like you're knocking on a door. A ripe watermelon will have a hollow sound instead of a "ping." Also, when a watermelon is ripe the side that is on the ground changes from white to yellow, and the two curly tendrils near the stem turn from green to brown.

Cantaloupes need to be picked when they're just right. When the bumpy lines on the skin become hard and lose their green color, gently pick up the melon. If it's ripe, it will come off the stem easily. If not, you need to wait a few days. But check often—you don't want to miss it.

Garden peas

Potatoes

Potatoes

Planting potatoes is like burying a treasure, only this treasure multiplies before you dig it up again. Make sure you have prepared your soil well before planting. Potatoes must have good soil.

When to plant. In early spring, as soon as the ground can be dug.

How to plant. Potatoes are usually planted from the "eyes" in seed potatoes. Seed potatoes are grown specially for gardeners, and you can buy them from a nursery, feed store, or catalog. Eyes are the little white bumps on the outside of the potato. They are the part that grows to be a potato plant.

A seed potato will have one or several eyes, depending on how big it is. Cut the seed potato into chunks about 2 inches wide. (Ask a grown-up for help if you need it.) Make sure each chunk has at least one eye.

Dig a ditch 12 inches deep. Then plant the chunks 2 to 4 inches deep in the bottom of your ditch, leaving 12 inches between chunks in the row. When the potato plant grows to the top of the ditch, pile soil or mulch around the stem so that only the top 2 or 3 inches is showing.

Grow in containers? Plant in a large, deep pot filled halfway with soil. When the potato plants reach the top of the pot, fill it almost all the way up with soil.

When to harvest. You can start digging up small kinds of potatoes (often called "new potatoes") when the plants start to flower. Large kinds of potatoes are dug when the plant starts to die down in the middle of the summer. If your soil is nice and loose, you can dig potatoes with your hands. If not, ask a grown-up for help digging them with a spading fork.

Pumpkins

Growing your own pumpkin for Halloween is a fun project. You'll need lots of room, because pumpkin vines sprawl all over the place. You'll also need to keep your plants well watered and fertilized.

Pumpkin

When to plant. After the last spring frost.

How to plant. Plant seeds 1 to 1½ inches deep and 30 inches apart. You need 6 to 10 feet between rows! Or plant in mounds, as described on page 72 for melons. Seeds will sprout in 6 to 10 days.

Grow in containers? No, even the smallest kinds need more room.

When to harvest. Pumpkins are ready when they turn bright orange, usually about 2½ to 4 months after you plant the seeds. Pick them when the vines start dying but before you get a hard frost. Store pumpkins in a cool, dry place until you want to use them.

Radishes

Some kinds of radishes can go from seeds to your salad in only 3 weeks!

When to plant. Six to 8 weeks before the last frost in spring. For a fall crop, plant in early fall.

How to plant. Plant in rows or scatter seeds, covering them with about ½ inch of soil. Seeds sprout in 3 to 10 days. Thin the seedlings so they are 1 to 2 inches apart.

Grow in containers? Yes.

When to harvest. Most radishes are ready 30 days after you plant the seeds, or even sooner. Start pulling when they are about 1 inch across. (Pull one up to check.)

Radishes

Squash

There are two kinds of squash, summer squash and winter squash. Summer squash has a thin skin that you eat. Zucchini is a summer squash. Winter squash usually has a hard shell. The part you eat is sweet and yellow.

Summer squash grows on bushy plants with big leaves and tiny little thorns on the stems. (Just one plant will give you *lots* of zucchini.) Winter squash grows on vine-like plants like its cousin the pumpkin.

When to plant. In spring after the last frost, for both kinds.

How to plant. Plant seeds 1 inch deep. Thin summer squash plants to 16 to 24 inches apart. Grow winter squash in mounds like those described on page 72 for melons. Leave 6 to 10 feet between mounds.

Grow in containers? Summer squash can be grown in a large container, but both kinds are really best in the ground.

When to harvest. Pick your first summer squash when they get to be 3 to 6 inches long (or several inches across for the round kind)—about 1½ to 2 months after planting the seeds. They taste best when they are small. Use a knife to cut the stem just above where it turns into the squash. (Ask a grown-up for help.)

Pick winter squash when the vines have started to die in the fall but before a heavy frost. The skins should be very hard. You can store winter squash in a cool, dry place all winter long.

Strawberries

If you want to see just how delicious fruit can be, try growing strawberries. You can grow lots in a half-barrel, sold in garden stores.

When to plant. In early spring, also late fall where winters are mild.

How to plant. Berries are sweetest when grown in plenty of sun, but where summers are really hot it's okay if they are shaded in the afternoon.

Summer squash

Plant 6 to 8 everbearing strawberry plants in each barrel. ("Everbearing" means they produce fruit all summer long instead of all at once in the spring.) Make sure not to bury the crown (the swollen part where the leaves come from), or the plant might rot.

Your berries will need to be watered and fertilized often. When the plants get older they will start to grow runners, which are long stems that have a new plant at the end. Cut these runners off, or your pot will get too crowded. However, after 3 or 4 years, your plants will start to get tired. Then you can let the new plants at the ends of the runners grow and take out the old plants.

Grow in containers? Definitely.

When to harvest. Strawberries are ready to pick when they are bright red from top to bottom.

Tomatoes

If you only have room for one vegetable, it should probably be a tomato. Tomatoes grow great in containers, and one plant will produce all summer long. Some kinds of tomatoes are so sweet that they taste like candy.

Tomatoes are so easy to grow that they are often put in cages so they don't get *too* wild. Well, sort of. Many tomatoes need help holding themselves up off the ground, so you can either tie them to stakes or buy or make a tomato cage—like a fence wrapped around the branches. (Find out about plant stakes and cages on page 45.)

When to plant. After the last spring frost.

How to plant. Set out seedlings 18 to 36 inches apart. Plant them so that only the top few leaves are above the soil.

Grow in containers? Definitely. Many short varieties don't need staking and are just right for containers.

When to harvest. Tomatoes can take anywhere from about 2 to 3 months from transplant to harvest, depending on what kind you plant. Start picking when the tomato is brightly colored.

A Green-bean Hideout

WHAT YOU NEED

8 bamboo or other thin poles, 6 to 8 feet tall

Roll of heavy twine

Package of scarlet runner or other pole bean seeds

On a hot summer day, what could be better than to duck into a cool and leafy hideout for a secret meeting with your friends, or for some time by yourself to read a favorite book or write in your garden journal?

Here's a kind of hideout you can actually grow from bean seeds! You'll need a circle of ground about 5 feet wide in a sunny part of your garden. You'll also need a friend or a grown-up assistant to help you set up the poles for the beans to climb on.

1 In the spring when there's no danger of frost, use a stick to draw a 5-foot-wide circle in the soil to mark where your bean tent should be. Prepare the soil around this line according to the instructions on page 23.

2 With a helper, push the ends of the poles into the ground all around your circle and lean them together at the top, like a tepee. Space them as evenly as you can—about 2 feet apart. (Leave a little extra space on one side for a doorway.)

3 Tie the tops of the poles together with twine, wrapping it over, under, and around the ends of the poles as many times as you need to so they won't come apart.

4 To give your bean plants plenty of surface to climb onto, you can make twine "poles" in between your wooden poles. First tie string to one side of your doorway near the bottom of the frame, then pull it tight and wind it around each pole until you get all the way around to the other side of the doorway. Don't tie any across your doorway! Now tie pieces of string between every two poles from the top of the frame to the string circle at the bottom.

5 Poke holes 1 to 2 inches deep about every 3 to 6 inches all the way around except right in front of your doorway. Plant a bean seed in each hole and cover it up with soil.

6 Gently water the seeds.

If you water your seeds faithfully and keep weeds pulled, you'll have seedlings in a couple of weeks. Once they're about 2 inches tall, thin them to 6 inches apart. Water and fertilize your plants regularly (see pages 36 to 38), and they will probably cover the frame with their leafy vines in a couple of months. In another month or so, bright red scarlet runner flowers will bloom. Soon you'll see beans!

Be sure to check for beans both inside and outside of your tent. Read about beans on page 70 to figure out when yours are ready to pick.

Basil

Chives

Dill

Mint

Oregano

Parsley

Herbs

Have you ever thought about why pizza tastes like pizza? Or why a dill pickle is so delicious? It's because of the herbs that give them their special tastes. Herbs are certain plants that we use to flavor our foods. Some herbs are also used for medicine, or for their nice smell. (By the way, "herbs" is pronounced as if it didn't have an "h" in front—you say "erbs.")

Most nurseries sell herb seeds and herbs in small containers. If you really want to see how many different types of herbs you can grow, send for a catalog from a company that specializes in herbs (see page 94).

When to plant them

Some herbs don't mind cold weather, but others do. The best bet is to plant after the last spring frost. That way your plants will grow quickly and you can begin using them soon. In mild-winter areas, herbs that don't mind the cold can also be planted in fall.

Where to plant them

Most herbs grow best in plenty of sun and average garden soil. They also are great in containers. In fact, many gardeners bring them indoors to a sunny window at the end of the summer.

How to grow them

There's nothing hard about growing herbs. Most kinds just need occasional watering, and you usually don't even have to fertilize them.

When most herb plants begin to bloom, it's time to use pruning shears to cut off about the top ⅓ of the stems. Ask an adult to help you.

How to harvest them

Herbs can be used fresh from the plant, or they can be dried to use later. To dry your herbs, cut long branches and hang them upside down in a cool, dark place. Once they're all dried out, pull the leaves off and put them in jars with tight-fitting lids. You can give some as presents to people who like to cook.

Some herbs to grow

There are many kinds of herbs you can grow. Here are a few to start with.

Basil. The dark green leaves of this plant are used in many Italian recipes. Basil gets to be about 1 to 2 feet high. Plant it again each spring.

Chives. This plant's grass-like, dark green leaves taste like onions. They are chopped up to flavor baked potatoes and other foods. Plant chives from bulbs in spring or fall, or from seedlings in spring. They grow about 1 to 2 feet tall.

Dill. The leaves, the lacy-looking flowers, and the seeds of the dill plant are used to season many foods—including dill pickles. To gather the seeds, tie a paper bag over the flower when it's almost dry. When you can hear the seeds shaking around in the bag, cut off the branch and take the seeds out. It's best to replant dill each spring. It grows easily from seed, and it can get to be more than 6 feet tall.

Mint. You already know some kinds of mint, like peppermint and spearmint. But did you know about pineapple mint, apple mint, and orange bergamot mint? Each kind has its own special flavor—try a few leaves in lemonade or tea.

Mints are pretty plants that like lots of water. In fact, if mint gets enough water it may spread into places you don't want it. Plant it in a container to keep it under control. Mints will grow in bright sun or a little shade. They can live through mild winters, but you need to plant them each year where winters are cold.

Oregano. This herb is one of the main flavorings in pizza and spaghetti sauce. Its tiny green leaves grow on plants that get to be about 2 or 3 feet high. Keep the flowers picked. Oregano will live through the winter in most places.

Parsley. Many people use parsley to decorate other foods. It makes everything look good! Parsley is wonderful in salads and soups, too.

The plant is bright green, with lacy or crinkly leaves that are best used fresh. It grows about a foot high. When parsley starts to bloom, let it—the flowers are loved by ladybugs and other good garden bugs. Plant parsley each spring, or in the fall if you live where winters don't get very cold.

Bulbs

Bulbs are easy-to-grow plants that rest underground for much of the year. When conditions are just right—usually when the soil starts to get warm in spring—they push their leaves up out of the soil and make beautiful flowers. Many bulbs will bloom over and over again for years.

There are hundreds of different kinds of bulbs and bulb-like plants. Some, like tulip and daffodil bulbs, look a lot like onions. Others, like some kinds of iris, look more like a piece of root.

Most bulbs are sold in garden stores either in fall or in early spring. There are also catalogs that specialize in selling bulbs. (See page 94.)

Many bulbs make beautiful cut flowers for bouquets. But most aren't like annual flowers that make more flowers when you cut some off. When you cut off a bulb blossom, it won't make another one until the next year.

When to plant them

Bulbs that can live where winters are cold and snowy, such as daffodils, should be planted in the fall. Some bulbs, such as gladiolus, like warmer weather; you plant them in the spring. If you live in an area that has cold winters and you want to grow bulbs that like it warm, you can dig them up in the fall before it gets too cold and store them in a dry place indoors until planting time the next spring.

Where to plant them

Since bulbs hide underground for much of the year, you can plant them just about anywhere. When the time is right, they'll grow and bloom. You can even plant bulbs under other flowers, such as pansies. The bulbs will just push their way to the top when it's time.

Most bulbs like sunny places, but some grow well in shade. You can also plant many bulbs in pots. Some will even grow indoors.

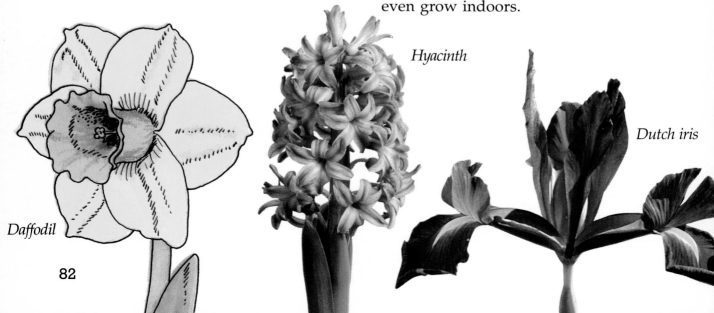

Hyacinth

Dutch iris

Daffodil

How to grow them

Turn to page 28 to see how to plant your bulbs in the ground, or to page 31 to see how to plant them in containers. Be sure to keep the soil moist all the time until the bulb is finished blooming.

Some easy bulbs to grow

These bulbs are almost foolproof:

Crocus. These tiny plants have little cup-shaped flowers that are white, yellow, or purple. They bloom so early in spring that they sometimes come up through the snow! You can also plant crocus indoors in small pots.

Daffodils & narcissus. Sunny yellow or white flowers bloom from daffodil and narcissus bulbs in early spring. Some daffodils grow only a few inches tall, and other kinds may be 2 feet tall. Strong-smelling paper-white narcissus bulbs are especially good for growing indoors.

Dutch iris. These tall, delicate-looking flowers come in shades of blue, red, pink, purple, yellow, and white. They are great to cut and put in a vase.

Hyacinths. Each hyacinth bulb sends up a beautiful spike of white, pink, or purple flowers. The blossoms have a wonderful sweet fragrance.

Tulips. These bulbs bloom in early spring, in lots of different colors. They do best where winters are frosty or cold.

Tulips

Crocus

83

A Never-ending Garden

Do you ever wish you could keep a little bit of your garden to look at forever? Pressing your favorite flowers, leaves, and grasses lets you do just that! You can use them to make an album of garden memories. Or you can make note cards, pictures for framing, bookmarks, and even place mats.

Flat flowers such as pansies press very well. Delicate flowers such as forget-me-nots look nice pressed in sprigs with their leaves and stems attached. You can also press individual flower petals. Choose some leaves, ferns, and grasses, too.

Your plants will press best when they are fresh, so have your pressing materials ready before you cut anything. Choose flowers and leaves that are dry and as perfect as possible, without bruises or tears. Use scissors to cut them.

1 Stack up 4 paper towels on a piece of cardboard. Carefully arrange as many plants as you can fit onto the top towel without crowding them. All the plants in one layer should be about the same thickness so they will press evenly.

2 Carefully stack 4 more paper towels over your plants, and then put another piece of cardboard on top.

3 Keep making layers of paper towels, plants, more paper towels, and cardboard until you have used up all your plants.

4 Put the stack in a warm, dry place and set bricks or books on top. Your plants will take 2 or 3 weeks to dry. Carefully check the top layer after a couple of weeks.

WHAT YOU NEED

Scissors

Flowers, leaves, and grasses

Roll of heavy-duty paper towels

Several pieces of heavy cardboard (about the size of a paper towel)

Bricks or heavy books

Heavy paper for gluing plants onto (try different colors and textures)

Thin metal pancake turner

White glue

Toothpicks

Tweezers

Clear plastic adhesive shelf paper (sold at hardware and variety stores)

Gluing your plants to paper

When your plants are completely dry, you can use them to make pictures on paper. Don't worry if every petal isn't perfect. You can even cut and rearrange petals, stems, and leaves if you want to.

1 Cut your paper to the size you want. For a note card, cut it twice as wide as you want the card to be so you can fold it in half. Or you can glue your flowers onto a smaller piece of paper in a different color and then glue that to the folded note card.

2 Very gently lift the paper towels off the top layer of dried plants. If the plants stick to the towels, use a pancake turner to carefully lift them off.

3 Pick up the plants with tweezers and arrange them on the paper until you like the way they look.

4 Squirt some glue onto a piece of paper towel. Then dip a toothpick into the glue, pick up a plant with tweezers, and put tiny dots of glue on the back of it. Lay the plant where you want it on the paper and press very lightly to make it stick. Do this for each piece of plant.

5 Let the glued plants dry several hours or until the next day.

6 When your work is completely dry, you can protect it by covering it with clear adhesive paper. (You don't need to do this for anything you are going to frame behind glass.)

If you are making a note card, cut a piece of the adhesive paper a little bigger than your folded card. Peel off the backing and center the clear paper over the card. Then place it on the card and smooth it from the center outward. Use scissors to trim off the extra.

If you are making a place mat, it's a good idea to cover both front and back with the adhesive paper. Cover the front side first, leaving about an inch extra all around. Lay this on another piece of adhesive paper, sticky sides together, and trim the edges close to the place mat.

Flowers

There are thousands of kinds of flowers that you can grow. Most are called either "annuals" or "perennials." Annual flowers live for one growing season, then make seeds and die. Each year you start with fresh seeds or new plants. Perennial flowers live for a long time, blooming year after year.

When to plant them

You can grow some kind of flower almost anytime. If you want your plants to bloom as long as possible, though, there are planting times that are best. Where winters are mild, plant perennial flowers in the fall or early spring. Where winters get very cold, plant them in spring after the last frost.

Annual flowers are like vegetables. Some like cool weather, and others like to be hot. Cool-loving annuals, like pansies and calendulas, are usually planted in very early spring or early fall so they can bloom before it gets too hot. Where winters are mild, many cool-loving annuals will even bloom in winter if you plant them in the fall. As the weather gets warmer in summer, cool-loving annuals stop blooming.

Warm-loving annuals, such as marigolds and zinnias, are planted after the last spring frost. They will bloom all summer long.

Where to plant them

Some flowers like to grow in shady places, and others like to have sun all day. Other than that, you can plant flowers almost anywhere you have room. Most flowers grow well in containers, too.

If you are planting many different types of flowers, keep the shortest kinds in the front of your flower garden or along the edge of the pot. That way they won't hide the ones in back.

How to grow them

Just follow the basic rules of good gardening—prepare the soil well before you plant, water and fertilize regularly, and keep the weeds pulled. Cut off faded flowers. (Read about that on page 44.) Some tall flowers will need to be staked so that they don't fall over in the wind. (Look on page 45 to see how to do that.)

COLOR A CARNATION

Here's a way to see how plants drink water. Fill a glass or vase halfway with water and add food coloring to turn the water a bright color. Now put the stem of a white carnation or other white flower in the water. In a few hours your flower will change color!

BLUE FOOD COLORING

Calendulas

Flowers to cut for bouquets

A bouquet of fresh flowers makes the inside of your house beautiful. Flowers that grow on long stems are usually best to cut for bouquets, but you can try almost anything. See page 46 for tips on cutting flowers.

Fun flowers to grow

There are so many wonderful kinds of flowers to grow that it's hard to choose! Here are some good ones.

Calendulas. It's easy to grow these bright yellow or orange annual flowers from either seeds or seedlings. Calendula plants grow 1 to 2 feet high, and they like plenty of sun. The flowers bloom in late winter to early spring. Where winters don't get very cold, you can plant calendulas in fall and you'll have winter flowers.

Carnations & cottage pinks. These two kinds of flowers are the most famous members of a large family of plants called *Dianthus*. They are perennials that have a nice spicy smell when their white, pink, or red flowers bloom in late spring or summer. Start with seedlings in the fall or early spring. Give these plants plenty of sun, and don't water them too much.

Coleus

Coleus. This annual is grown for its colorful leaves instead of its flowers. It grows best in shady gardens and makes a good indoor plant, too. Start with seedlings after the last frost in spring. In fall, take cuttings from your plants (see how on page 60) and grow new coleus plants indoors over winter. When coleus starts to bloom, pinch off the flowers so the plant will make more pretty leaves instead.

Cosmos. Flowers shaped like daisies bloom on this annual plant all summer long. The flowers come in white and bright pink, red, purple, and orange. Cosmos plants grow quickly, and some kinds reach 8 feet tall. Plant them in a sunny spot where there is plenty of room to grow. You can start with seeds or seedlings after the last spring frost.

Impatiens. If your garden is shady, this is one of the best annuals for you. The little round blossoms come in lots of colors, bright as lollipops. Impatiens plants usually get to be 6 to 12 inches high, and they are especially nice to grow in a hanging pot. Start with seedlings after the last spring frost.

Marigolds. It's hard to miss with this sturdy annual. Marigolds love the heat of summer. Start with either seeds or seedlings, and plant them in a sunny spot after the last spring frost. The flowers come in yellow, orange, and reddish brown. Some marigolds only get to be 6 inches high, and some are taller than 3 feet.

Pansies & violas. These spring-blooming annuals have flowers that look like little faces. Some are all one color, and others come in a combination of colors. Pansies have bigger flowers—up to 3 inches across. Viola flowers are about half that size, but there are usually more of them. Plants get about 6 to 12 inches high. Start with seedlings in early spring, or in fall if you live where winters don't get very cold. Plant them in bright sun or just a little shade.

Impatiens

Marigolds

Pansy

Cosmos

Petunias. You can choose almost any color of petunia flower to grow—even stripes! The blossoms are shaped like little trumpets. These annual plants usually reach 1 to 2 feet high. Start with seedlings after the last frost in spring. Petunias will bloom all summer long in a nice sunny spot.

Snapdragons. When you pinch the sides of a snapdragon blossom, it opens and shuts like the mouth of a dragon! Snapdragons are grown as annuals even though they can live through the winter where the weather is very mild. The flowers come in lots of colors.

Petunias

Snapdragons grow 1 to 3 feet tall, depending on what kind you choose. Start with seedlings in early spring, and plant them where they'll get lots of sun.

Sunflowers. These annuals are the sky-scrapers of the flower world, sometimes growing more than 10 feet tall! The yellow edges of the large flowers make them look like the sun. Sunflowers like lots of sun, frequent fertilizer, and regular watering. Plant seeds after the last spring frost in a spot where they'll have plenty of room.

When the flowers dry you can eat the seeds or feed them to birds. Cut off the flower when it is almost dry. Let it dry out completely in the sun. Then remove the seeds and store them in a cool, dry place.

Sunflower

Sweet peas. You're planting perfume when you grow these annual flowers—they have a wonderfully sweet smell. Sweet peas grow on vines and bloom in the spring in almost every color.

Start sweet peas from either seeds or seedlings in early spring. Most sweet pea plants like to climb, so you'll need to plant them next to a trellis. (Read how to make a trellis on page 45.) Or you can plant a short bush variety that won't need a trellis. Plant sweet peas in a sunny location in early spring, or in fall in mild-winter areas. Water them regularly.

Zinnias. For one of summer's best annual flowers to cut for bouquets, grow zinnias. They have long stems and blossoms that come in lots of bright colors. Some are huge with ruffly petals, and others are like little buttons. Some grow 4 feet tall, others just a foot. You can start with either seeds or seedlings after the last frost in spring. Plant them in a sunny spot.

Sweet peas

DRY A BOUQUET

Some flowers can be dried and made into everlasting bouquets. A few good flowers to grow for this are celosia, strawflower, cornflower, yarrow, and gomphrena. Cut the flowers when blossoms are about halfway to ¾ open. Then hang them upside down in a cool, dark place. When they are completely dry, make a bouquet. You don't have to put it in water!

Zinnias

Plants You Can Pet

Some plants just feel good when you touch them. Maybe they have soft, velvety leaves, so that touching them is like petting a cat. Or maybe they feel kind of tickly. Some plants smell great when they are touched, too. Grow "feely" plants where you can touch them often. You can also plant them in pots.

Here are some good plant "pets." Nurseries sell these plants in cell-packs, 4-inch pots, or 1-gallon cans.

Lamb's ears. The woolly gray leaves of this plant feel as soft as a lamb's ear! In midsummer it has swirly purple flowers. Plant lamb's ears in bright sun or part shade. It needs less water than most plants, but don't let it dry out completely.

Scented geraniums. The leaves of these plants smell nice when you touch or crush them. Some smell like lime, others like apples, nutmeg, or roses. Peppermint-scented geranium also has soft, velvety leaves.

Scented geraniums have colorful flowers in spring. They grow best in lots of sun or in part shade, with regular watering. They won't live through cold winters.

Sea pink. This plant looks kind of like grass, with little pink flower balls in spring. It grows best in plenty of sun, and it doesn't need a lot of water. Try growing some in a pot, drawing a face on the pot, and letting the sea pink be the hair for the face. You can give it a haircut, and it will grow back!

Irish & Scotch moss. These dainty little plants look and feel as soft and cool as any plant there is. Mosses like lots of sun or just a little shade, and regular water.

Sea pink

Irish moss

Houseplants

Growing houseplants is like bringing a little bit of the outdoors inside. Not all plants grow well indoors—most kinds you see outside need more light. But there are lots of plants that will do fine inside your house.

Garden stores sell many kinds of houseplants, big and small. Most florist shops also sell houseplants, and so do many supermarkets. Some places sell blooming plants, such as azaleas and chrysanthemums, to keep indoors for a week or two. But eventually these plants need to be taken outside or they will die. Few plants bloom well indoors.

When to plant them

You can plant houseplants anytime.

Where to grow them

All houseplants need light from outdoors, so the best place for them is close to a sunny window. The important thing to know is just how close to the window they should be. Some houseplants, like coleus, will thrive right in a sunny window. But most do best if the sun doesn't shine right on them. They like to be away from the window a bit, or near a window where the sun doesn't shine straight through. Keep them away from drafty places or heating vents, too.

How to grow them

Houseplants need to be watered and fertilized. Read pages 50 to 54 to see how to do this, and to see what to do when a plant gets too big for its pot.

Some easy-to-grow houseplants

These plants all grow well indoors. It's fun to make "baby" plants from some of them—turn to page 57 to learn how.

Bromeliads. If you like kind of weird plants, try bromeliads. They are also one of the few kinds of houseplants that bloom well indoors. Sometimes the leaves are bright colored, too.

In nature bromeliads are "epiphytes," which means they grow in the air attached to the sides of tree branches. Many people grow them on little

Bromeliads

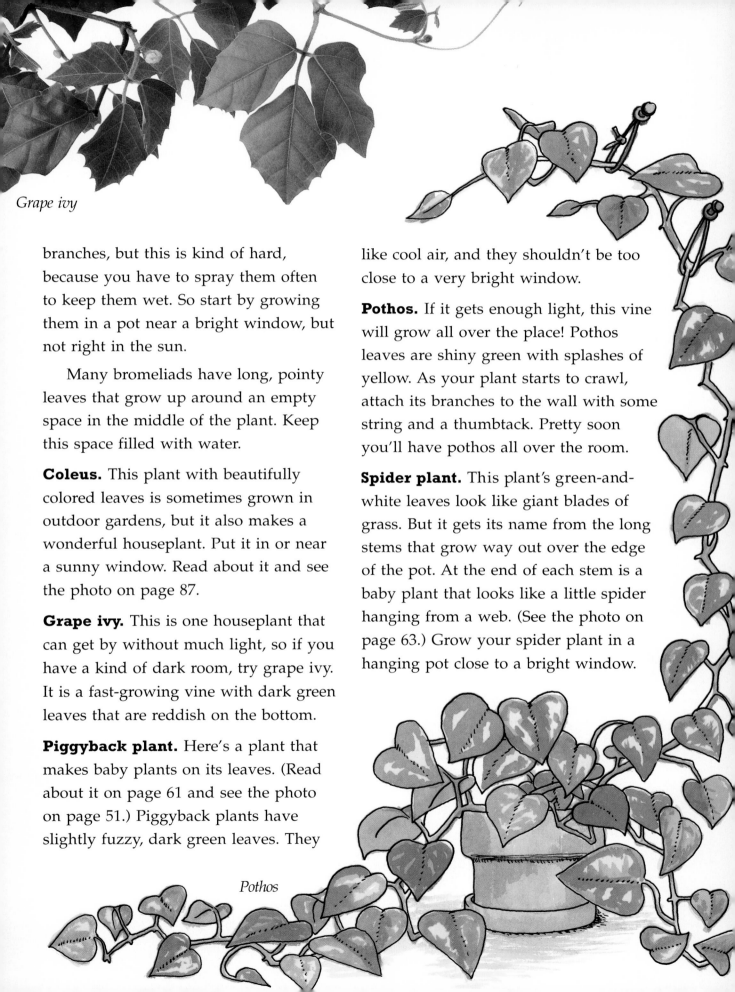

Grape ivy

branches, but this is kind of hard, because you have to spray them often to keep them wet. So start by growing them in a pot near a bright window, but not right in the sun.

Many bromeliads have long, pointy leaves that grow up around an empty space in the middle of the plant. Keep this space filled with water.

Coleus. This plant with beautifully colored leaves is sometimes grown in outdoor gardens, but it also makes a wonderful houseplant. Put it in or near a sunny window. Read about it and see the photo on page 87.

Grape ivy. This is one houseplant that can get by without much light, so if you have a kind of dark room, try grape ivy. It is a fast-growing vine with dark green leaves that are reddish on the bottom.

Piggyback plant. Here's a plant that makes baby plants on its leaves. (Read about it on page 61 and see the photo on page 51.) Piggyback plants have slightly fuzzy, dark green leaves. They

like cool air, and they shouldn't be too close to a very bright window.

Pothos. If it gets enough light, this vine will grow all over the place! Pothos leaves are shiny green with splashes of yellow. As your plant starts to crawl, attach its branches to the wall with some string and a thumbtack. Pretty soon you'll have pothos all over the room.

Spider plant. This plant's green-and-white leaves look like giant blades of grass. But it gets its name from the long stems that grow way out over the edge of the pot. At the end of each stem is a baby plant that looks like a little spider hanging from a web. (See the photo on page 63.) Grow your spider plant in a hanging pot close to a bright window.

Pothos

Shopping for Your Garden

You can shop for plants and gardening equipment at special garden stores called "nurseries," or you can shop through the mail by ordering from gardening catalogs. You can learn a lot either way, even if you aren't buying a lot.

A nursery is sort of a supermarket for gardeners. It sells plants and seeds, tools, pots, potting soil, fertilizers, and all sorts of other gardening supplies. Usually the people who work at nurseries have studied plants, so they can answer your gardening questions.

Sometimes big hardware stores or variety stores also have garden departments where you can buy plants and gardening equipment.

Shopping by mail

Mail-order catalogs are a good way to learn about plants. Many of them have beautiful color photographs, and they all offer plants that you may not see anywhere else.

When you order from a catalog, check to see when the plants will be sent. This information is usually in the front of the catalog or near the order form. If you know when your plants will be coming, you can have your garden all ready for planting. (Most mail-order plants should be planted right away.) And you won't be disappointed by having to wait a lot longer than you expected.

Plants sent through the mail are usually small. Their size may be a little disappointing, but they'll grow fast. Besides, small plants cost less to mail.

Here are some catalogs you can send away for. Unless a price is listed, the catalogs are free.

Breck's
P.O. Box 1757
Peoria, IL 61656
Colorful catalog with all types of bulbs.

Jackson & Perkins Co.
P.O. Box 1028
Medford, OR 97501

Beautiful color catalogs of roses, fruit, bulbs, and perennial flowers.

K. Van Bourgondien & Sons, Inc.
P.O. Box 1000
Babylon, NY 11702

Specializes in bulbs and also sells fruit, perennials, and houseplants.

Nichols Garden Nursery, Inc.

1190 N. Pacific Highway

Albany, OR 97321

Herb seeds and plants, also vegetables and flowers.

Park Seed Company, Inc.

Cokesbury Rd.

North Greenwood, SC 29646

Annual flower and vegetable seeds, also bulbs, herbs, and garden supplies.

Seeds Blüm

Idaho City Stage

Boise, ID 83706

One of the most interesting catalogs. Sells "heritage" (old-time) vegetables, many with special stories of their own. Catalog $3.

Thompson & Morgan

P.O. Box 1308

Jackson, NJ 08527

Huge selection of all kinds of flower and vegetable seeds. Lots of helpful information.

W. Atlee Burpee Company

300 Park Ave.

Warminster, PA 18974

Annual flower and vegetable seeds, also fruit and berry plants, herbs, and garden supplies.

Wayside Gardens

1 Garden Way

Hodges, SC 29695

A fun catalog with all kinds of perennial flowers and other plants.

Well-Sweep Herb Farm

317 Mt. Bethel Rd.

Port Murray, NJ 07865

A large selection of herb plants and things made out of herbs. If you're in New Jersey, it's also a great place to visit. Catalog $2.

White Flower Farm

P.O. Box 50

Litchfield, CT 06759

Many types of flowering plants. The pictures and plant descriptions make it worth the cost. Catalog $5.

Soil testing by mail

If you want to have soil tested for lead but can't find a testing lab, here are two that are less expensive than many. Call or write to make sure of the price and to find out how to collect your soil sample. Read about lead testing on page 21.

Coffey Laboratories, Inc.

12423 N.E. Whitaker Way

Portland, OR 97230

Telephone: (503) 254-1794

The price at the time this book was printed was $20.

Soil Testing Lab

West Experiment Station

University of Massachusetts

Amherst, MA 01003

Telephone: (413) 545-2311

The price at the time this book was printed was $7. The lab says its test is less accurate for lead content if you have alkaline soil.

Sunset
Proof-of-Purchase
ISBN 0-376-03076

Index